P9-DHI-062

THE POWER OF DETERMINATION

 THE TOWNSEND LIBRARY

THE POWER OF DETERMINATION

TP THE TOWNSEND LIBRARY

For more titles in the Townsend Library,
visit our website: www.townsendpress.com

Copyright © 2017 by Townsend Press
Printed in the United States of America

0 9 8 7 6 5 4 3 2

Townsend Press, Inc.
439 Kelley Drive
West Berlin, NJ 08091
cs@townsendpress.com

ISBN-13: 978-1-59194-503-1

Library of Congress Control Number:
2016920068

Contents

Acknowledgments

"Maria," "Erika," "Jeroboam," "Indonesia and Ericka," "Melissa," "Tricia," "Richard," "Crystal," by Beth Johnson. Photos courtesy of Beth Johnson.

"Paul," by Paul Langan. Photo courtesy of Eliza A. Comodromos.

"Tay Thi," by Nicholas Kristof. Originally published as "Graduate of the Year" in *The New York Times*, May 25, 2014. Reprinted by permission of PARS International. Photo courtesy of Room to Read.

"Peter," by Bob Johnson. Photo courtesy of Bob Johnson.

"Suashunn," by Beth Johnson. Photo courtesy of Isaac Ruth.

"Juan," by Juan Angel. Photo courtesy of Juan Angel.

"Amanda," by Robert Miedel. Photo courtesy of Amanda Patterson.

Introduction

John Langan

The Power of Determination tells the stories of fourteen people who carry the following belief in their hearts:

> I have taken charge of my life. I am determined to do what is needed to grow and succeed in life. I will let nothing stop me. In the face of obstacles, I will persist. When I get knocked down, I'll get back up.
>
> I believe in the words of the late fighter Muhammad Ali: "I hated every minute of training, but I said, 'Don't quit. Suffer now and live the rest of your life as a champion.'"

All the stories in this collection are about people with commitment, determination, and resolve. All of them remind me of an influential English teacher I had during my senior year in high school:

Mr. Gery started his first class with us by placing on the front desk a large mound of clay and, next to it, a rock about the size of a tennis ball. That got our attention quickly, and the class quieted down and waited for him to talk.

He looked at us and smiled and said, "If there were a pill I could give you that would help you succeed, and help you want to succeed, I would pass it out right now. But there is no magic pill. Everything is up to you."

Then Mr. Gery held up his fist and kind of shook it at us. Some of us looked at each other. *What's going on?* we all thought. He continued: "I'd like you to imagine something for me. Imagine that my fist is the real world—not the sheltered world of this school, but the real world. Imagine that my fist is everything that can happen to you out in the real world."

Then he pointed down to the ball of clay and also the rock. He said, "Now imagine that you're either this lump of clay or you're the rock. Got that?" He smiled at us, and we waited to see what he was going to do.

He went on, "Let's say you're this ball of clay, and you're just sitting around minding your own business, and then, out of nowhere, here's what happens." He made a fist again, and he smashed his fist into the ball of clay, which quickly turned into a half-flattened lump.

He looked at us, still smiling. "If the real world comes along and takes a swing at you, you're likely to get squashed. And you know what, the real world *will* come along and take a swing at you. You're going to take some heavy hits. Maybe you already have taken some heavy hits. Chances are that there are more down the road. So if you don't want to get squashed, you're better off if you're not a piece of clay.

"Now let's say you're the rock, and the real world comes along and takes a swing at you. What will happen if I smash my fist into this rock?" The answer was obvious. Nothing would happen to the rock. It would take the blow and not be changed.

He continued, "So what would you like to be, people, the clay or the rock? And what's my point? What am I trying to say to you?"

Someone raised a hand and said, "We should all be rocks. It's bad news to be clay." And some of us laughed, though a bit uneasily.

He went on, "You know I can't be a fairy godmother. I can't pull out a wand and say, 'Thanks for wanting to be a rock. I hereby wave my wand and make you a rock.' That's not the way life works. The only way to become a rock is to go out and make yourself a rock.

"Imagine you're a fighter getting ready for a match. You go to the gym, and maybe when you start, your whole body is flab, and it's soft like the clay. To make your body hard like a rock, you've got to train.

"Now if you want to train and become hard like the rock, I can help you. I can help you learn the skills you need to acquire knowledge. But you know, I'm just a trainer. I can't make you be a fighter.

"All I can do is tell you that you need to make yourself a fighter. Don't spend your time just being Mr. Cool Man or Ms. Designer Clothes or Most Popular Person. BE SOMEONE!"

He then smashed that wad of clay one more time, and the thud of his fist broke the silence and then created more silence. He sure had our total attention.

"At the end of the semester, some of you are going to leave here, and you're still going to be clay. You're going to be the kind of person that life can smush around. But some of you are going to be rocks. I want you to be a rock. Go for it. And when this comes"—and he held up his fist—"you'll be ready."

As the semester unfolded, when someone would not hand in a paper and make a lame excuse, he would respond, "Whatever you say, Mr. Clay." Or if someone would forget a book, or not study for a test, or not do a reading assignment, he would say, "Of course, Ms. Clay."

Mr. Gery worked us very hard, but he was not a mean person. We all knew he was a kind man who wanted us to become strong. It was obvious he wanted us to do well. By the end of the semester, he had to call very few of us Mr. or Ms. Clay.

Along with the advice of Mr. Gery, I want to share with you the following seven thoughts. Read and think about them and see if they speak to anything in your soul.

Thought #1: Having a Dream

Several years ago, my wife and I were vacationing in New Mexico. As we drove into one small town, we suddenly came upon a huge billboard. I was so struck by what it said that I stopped our car and wrote down the words.

> **If you never have a dream, you'll never have a dream come *true*.**

You need to have a dream within you—a belief and resolve in your heart that you will take charge of your life and make yourself proud.

Take a minute to think about this question: Which would you rather be—someone who *wins* a million dollars or someone who's *earned* a million dollars? Of course, we'd all like to wake up one morning and learn that we've just won a million dollars. But let's face it: this isn't very likely. So if you're realistic, chances are you would choose to be the person who worked hard, overcame obstacles, and achieved success. If so, your attitude might be: "I'm going to work hard to succeed. At this stage in my life, that may mean doing well in school because education can be clearly a key to success." And if you've made mistakes in the past (and many of us have), your attitude should be: "I can change my behavior. I'm going to learn to work hard so I can get somewhere and be someone."

#2: Your Attitude about Learning

Think about your own attitude toward learning. Put a check by the item or items that apply to you. (If you agree with some sentences in an item but not others, cross out the ones you do not agree with.)

_____ School has never really turned me on. I feel I can start to study if I need to, but I don't want to. What's wrong with being a bit lazy? Life is supposed to be about enjoying yourself and having some fun. I want to take it easy and have as much good time as I can for now.

_____   I suppose I am passive about studying, but it's not all my fault. I'm tired of being told what to do. I'm tired of being force-fed what other people think I need to learn. A lot of the stuff is not going to be of any value to me as far as I can see. I can't wait to get out of school and be on my own so I can start living my life.

_____   If I study too much, I'll miss out on the good times that school has to offer. I won't have time to go to games or parties. And I don't want to be alone. If I start studying, some of my friends are going to think twice about hanging out with me.

_____   I want to do more in school, but I'm afraid of really giving it a good effort. What if I try my best and I still get lousy grades? People will just laugh at me. I don't want to look foolish, so I'm probably just going to drift along and not call any attention to myself.

_____   I guess I've just been out of it for a long time. There are probably lots of reasons why. I never got any encouragement along the way. I pretty much just let things happen to me. I feel like a piece of driftwood that's been tossed about on a stormy sea. I do want to do something and to become someone. I've felt like this for a while, and at times I really want to get serious. But so far I just haven't done so.

_____   I'm not an active student who tries my best all the time. But I'm not a zombie either. I do some studying, just not as much as other people would like me to. I should probably do more, and I'm going to work on that and try to do a better job of taking charge of my studies.

_____   I feel something stirring within me. For a long time I was dead to learning, but now I want to get somewhere. I'm ready to be a serious student. It's true that some of the stuff I have to study is boring, and some teachers do not care. But I feel now that these are just hurdles that will not stop me. I'm going to start doing more to get where I want to go.

_____   I'm on the move, and I have taken charge of my life. There is something inside me that is strong and determined to succeed. I feel in my heart of hearts that nothing is going to stop me. It's my life, and I'm going to work hard and respect myself and gain success and happiness.

So where do you fit? The items above will help you think about what your attitude is and how you can improve it.

Thought #3: Doing the Work

When I was a teacher in a community college, I found that the key to a student's success was his or her *attitude*. Some students had made an inner commitment to doing the work needed to succeed. When the crunch would come—and the crunch is the plain hard work that is often required—the student with commitment would meet it head-on; the student without commitment would avoid it in a hundred different ways.

On the following scale of *Passive* to *Determined*, where would you rate yourself?

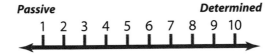

Why have you rated yourself as you have? What strengths can you build upon? What are the personal challenges you must overcome? Ideally, sit down and do a paper in which you write and think about these important questions.

Thought #4: An Unequal Playing Field

There is a popular idea in America that has always made me uneasy. It is the idea that success is within us—that we can all "pull ourselves up by our bootstraps" and triumph over tough odds.

Now there is truth to this idea, but it is not the whole truth. Life is like a race, and there are different lanes on the racetrack. Some of us are in lanes where there are no obstacles on the track. Some of us are in lanes where there are all kinds of obstacles—for example, personal health challenges, family neglect or abuse, poverty, racism, a neighborhood environment with violence and drugs, a school where one's peers are not into studies but into "respecting themselves" by being in the right clique, wearing the right kind of footwear, having the right hair style, or whatever.

If you're in a track that is full of obstacles, you can get worn down. You can start losing hope. And then I think it is harder to ignite the spark of determination within. To me, there is no question about what you must do in such circumstances: You must be a hero. You must battle the odds. You must keep alive a belief deep inside yourself that you can make your world a better one. And the first step in doing that is to know your life has been hard, but that you will not give up. If you have read this introduction so far, there is no question in my mind but that you can do it. You can be a fighter. You can be a hero. You can have the courage to inspire others. I believe you can do it. Can you?

Thought #5: A Quotation to Live By

If I could pass along one quotation, it would be this line from the great religious and political leader Mahatma Gandhi: **"Be the change you want to see in the world."** These ten words are all simple ones, but put together they express an idea with unlimited power. The key to changing your world is to take personal responsibility for your actions and behavior. No one else can do this for you; it must be you alone.

To put Gandhi's idea another way, each one of us has his or her own ship to sail. Some people don't sail their own ships; they just kind of drift with the tides. That's not a very satisfying way to live one's life, just drifting along with others who are also drifting, and yet a lot of people do it. If their friends and peers are into enjoying the moment and taking the easy way out and not into setting larger goals in life, that's what they do.

I urge you to actively sail your own ship. That ship of yours is unique and precious, and no one else should sail it for you. That ship is the journey of your life. You get to go on that journey only once, and it's a one-way ticket, so you want to make the most of it. Dream dreams, set meaningful goals, make something happen. Don't just drift along with the tides. Become someone.

Thought #6: The Fact of Loneliness

Perhaps the biggest reason it is so hard to take responsibility for one's life and sail one's own ship is the fear of being alone. No one wants to be alone, and small wonder. If no one seems to care for us, and if we don't have the strength that comes from respecting and loving ourselves, we might just shrivel up and die. Yet our greatest artists tell us that loneliness is a fundamental fact of the human condition. Here, for example, is an unforgettable line from the poet T.S. Eliot:

Each in his prison thinking of the key . . .

We are all inside ourselves, each with our own consciousness, and we so much want to find the key that will get us out to other people and let other people get in to us. Of course we do find ways to connect with and love each other, and those connections sustain us. But it is equally true that each of us remains in his or her own separate room of individual consciousness.

To grow, we must sometimes set sail in new directions and leave acquaintances and friends behind. At such times, we must have the courage and strength to depend on ourselves. We must be ready to handle the loneliness that may be part of marching to the beat of our own drummer. We must not cling to the crowd when it prevents our personal growth. When the adventurer Columbus set sail for America, it was a terrifying thing to do. But he discovered a new world, and if we have the courage to sail our own ship, so might we.

Thought #7: A Basic Truth about Human Nature

Consider this basic truth about human nature: we all want to respect ourselves. We all want to live our lives in such a way that we think well of our behavior and others think well of us. We do not want to be disrespected or seen as bad people. An equally basic truth is that the only way we can get respect is to earn it. What is important and meaningful is what we earn through trying hard and working hard.

I think we all succumb to a fantasy at times: the hope and belief that we will get something for nothing. But everyone knows from experience or in the deepest part of their heart that such a hope is a false one. Life seldom gives us something for nothing—how many people win the lottery? Life is demanding. And because this is so, to get somewhere and to become someone, we must be prepared and able to make a solid effort. We must accept the fact that little can be won or achieved or cherished in life without hard work. The decision that each of us must make is the commitment to do the hard work required for success in life. By making such a decision and acting on it, we assume control of our lives.

All of the stories on the pages that follow are about people who have assumed control of their lives. Despite whatever difficulties and obstacles they faced, they discovered a powerful determination inside themselves. They made a commitment to succeed—and they succeeded. It is my hope and belief that by reading their stories, you, too, will be inspired to pursue your dreams. ■

Maria

WHEN she graduated from Philadelphia's Moore College of Art and Design in the spring of 2016, Maria Sweeney spoke to the assembled graduates and their families. She was given this honor as the recipient of a women's leadership award.

Maria gave an inspiring speech about her "transformative experience" at the college. She praised the guidance and encouragement she had received from her instructors. She thanked the school for the exciting opportunities it had provided. She expressed appreciation for the ways Moore had developed her confidence "in myself as a woman in the arts, and simply as a woman."

It was a beautiful and heartfelt speech. And it was especially memorable because of what Maria did *not* mention.

"My condition is out there," she says today. "I can't hide it. I don't want to be known as 'that girl in the wheelchair.' I just want to be known as Maria."

And yet you can't really understand who Maria is—her strength, her determination, her remarkable courage—without knowing what she lives with every day.

Maria's story begins in the Eastern European country of Moldova, where she was born 22 years ago. It was clear from the beginning that Maria had physical problems. She was diagnosed with a condition in which the body's joints don't move normally and may even be stuck in one position. Her feet rotated inward—a birth defect known as "club feet." Because Moldova did not have good medical care for a baby with special needs, her parents made the difficult decision to allow Maria to be adopted. Her new parents were the Sweeneys, a couple in a small New Jersey town. As time went on, Maria was joined by two adoptive siblings: Mariah (now 23), from Russia, and Nikita (now 15), from Ukraine.

As Maria grew and became more active, a frightening pattern emerged. When she would take a tumble that would not harm an ordinary child, Maria often broke a bone—or two. As they made repeated trips to the emergency room with their child, the Sweeneys worried that doctors would suspect they were abusing her. Fortunately, the family was able to turn to one of the best children's hospitals in the world: Nemours, the Alfred I. DuPont Hospital for Children in Wilmington, Delaware. Specialists at Nemours diagnosed Maria with a second condition known as "brittle bone disease." Just as the name suggests, people with this condition have very fragile bones that can break easily, sometimes for no apparent reason.

When Maria was 13, doctors came to another conclusion. They realized that both of her problems—the joint abnormalities and the brittle bones—were actually part of a single condition known as Bruck syndrome. Bruck syndrome is extremely rare; in fact, Maria is the only Bruck patient being treated at Nemours.

When Maria was younger, she kept count of her broken bones. As the number climbed, she lost interest in that game. She has been hospitalized more times than she can count. As a child, she had intravenous (IV) treatment that helped strengthen her bones. When she was 13, she had surgery to treat her scoliosis (curving of the spine). The treatment sounds like something out of a horror movie. A metal "halo" was installed around her head. (Small dents from the halo are still visible on her forehead.) Cables from the halo went up over a pulley and were attached to weights that gradually stretched Maria's neck. Every few days, more weight was added. After six weeks of this, doctors operated, installing a series of plates and screws in her upper spine to straighten and strengthen it. Afterward, Maria had to re-learn to walk.

It would be nice to say that throughout these ordeals, Maria had the support of a group of friends who loved and encouraged her. Sadly, that wasn't the case.

She attended a Catholic elementary school. "Academically, it was very good," she says. "I got a solid education." But socially, Maria struggled.

"I was different," Maria says. "The school wasn't at all diverse. I think there was one African-American student, and nobody but me had a disability you could see. Most of the other students were from wealthier families. My father was unemployed for a long period. We were that weird family who had adopted kids with physical problems. I was an easy target for teasing and bullying."

It is understandable that Maria's classmates, especially in the early elementary years, would be curious about this girl whose body looked different, who missed school because of hospitalizations, who sometimes needed a wheelchair or a walker to get around.

It is less understandable why the adults at the school didn't make an effort to educate the children about Maria's condition, and about "differences" in general.

Instead, Maria was left on her own.

"It was like there was a wall between me and the other kids," she remembers. "When I was in my wheelchair, they treated it like a toy; they wanted to play with it. They didn't seem to realize there was a person using it."

The idea that Maria's bones broke easily fascinated the other children. When she was in third grade, a classmate announced that she was going to trip Maria to see if it was really true.

She broke Maria's arm.

Maria tries to understand the mentality that was behind the girl's action. "She was young," Maria says today. "I know that she didn't really understand the consequences. But she was, frankly, a mean kid and a bully. She told me she would do it, and she did."

On another occasion, a student threw a backpack at Maria when she was sitting in the school bleachers. She fell to the ground, suffering more fractures.

Teachers were not deliberately abusive, but they could be as clueless as their students. When Maria was in fourth grade, the school had a fire drill. At that time, she was using a walker. The drill required the students to cross an uneven stretch of ground. Maria knew she couldn't keep her balance in such a situation. She told her teacher, who responded, "Well, you'll just have to." She fell, ending up with both a broken arm and a broken leg.

While such experiences were miserable, they also helped to instill in Maria a fierce desire for independence. Her physical condition was a harsh reality that she was going to have to deal with on a daily basis. But she became determined that being "the girl with that weird syndrome" was not going to define her.

Maria moved on to a Catholic high school, where her experience was a happier one and she made some good friends. But her sister Mariah, who was in the same grade, persuaded their parents to allow them to finish their high-school studies online. Maria wasn't happy about the decision at first, but she recognized that the school tuition was a hardship for her parents.

"And it turned out to be a blessing in

disguise," Maria says now. "In the course of those years, I discovered art."

On her own, Maria became fascinated with drawing and painting. She visited her local library again and again, checking out instructional art books. She sketched for hours, making tiny improvements with every version. In her online world, she found other people who loved art and encouraged her work.

As Maria's confidence in her abilities grew, so did her ambition. Her parents had assumed that Maria would attend the local community college and live at home. But she had other ideas. She became determined to become a professional artist and to make her own way in the world.

"I decided I was going to go to Moore," she said. "And I was going to live on my own, in Philadelphia."

Maria began working hard on putting together a portfolio (a collection of her art work) for Moore. Compared to most applicants, she was at a disadvantage. She was entirely self-taught. She had started late, while other students had had years of art classes. But to her delight, she was accepted, and she received a generous scholarship for low-income students with special needs.

Maria knew she needed to prepare for life in the dorm and in the city. In the summer before her freshman year, after having tendon surgery at Nemours, she went through "boot camp" with a physical therapist. Under the therapist's direction, she carried a heavy backpack, prepared for fire drills, and got ready for the physical realities she would face in college.

College was a wonderful experience for Maria. She lived in a dorm, interacted with her classmates, and polished her skills. She loved the experience of being in the city, with its wealth of cultural opportunities. She threw herself into her work-study job, which involved supervising a weekly live-model drawing session. She scheduled the models, arranged lights in the studio, and cleaned up afterward.

Over Christmas break during her freshman year, a happy new chapter opened in Maria's life. She was spending some time on Facebook when she noticed a spam folder she'd never realized was there. Most of the contents were junk, but there was also a year-old message from Eros Livieratos, a fellow New Jerseyite who had participated in Maria's online high-school program. Eros had come across some posts of Maria's, thought she was both interesting and cute, and sent her a friendly note—which had disappeared into the spam folder. "Naturally, I'd thought she was just ignoring me!" Eros says with a laugh.

Maria responded with an apologetic message, and the two began to talk via email and Skype. In January, Eros visited her at college. The two hit it off. Eros, a writer, was attending William Paterson College. Gradually their friendship grew and, as Maria says, "He became my boo!"

Not only is Eros Maria's "boo," but the two have become partners in an artistic endeavor: a comic book titled *In a Rut*. Eros writes the copy and Maria does the artwork in what they describe as stories based on "the New Jersey scene—flawed, burned out, punk kids." They are working on volume 2 of the series, which they sell at comic conventions and online. They have also adopted a rabbit, and Maria jokes about the two needing to save for "bunny college."

Maria's senior year in college was an extremely challenging one. By October of that year, she was using her wheelchair because of fractures in her femurs (the bones of the thigh). Over the holiday break, she had surgery at a Philadelphia hospital—not Nemours, where she had been seen so many times before. The surgery went very badly. She was left with an oversized metal plate in her knee, the edge of which can be felt through her skin; constant pain; and less ability to bend her knee than ever before. She was advised to take a semester off to recover, but she desperately wanted to graduate with her friends.

She wanted to walk across that stage to accept her diploma.

But as Maria has had to learn, wanting isn't getting.

Maria did graduate with her friends, but she did so in a wheelchair.

She spoke on the topic of leadership, but she gave the topic an unusual, and very meaningful, twist.

"What I talked about, basically, was leading myself," she says. "I've had to push myself to be where I am. I know a lot of college girls who've never even made their own doctor's appointments. I'm not criticizing them—they haven't had to. For me, making appointments, dealing with forms, procedures, insurance, scheduling surgeries, trying to coordinate rehab with my classes—those things are part of my life. They aren't all of my life. But they're things that I've needed to do in order to achieve the self-reliance I have always yearned for."

A month from now, Maria will undergo another surgery, this time at Nemours, that she hopes will correct the damage done by the previous operation. She admits to being "incredibly anxious" about it, but working daily on her comics and other art keeps her busy and focused.

When asked about her future hopes, Maria grows thoughtful.

"Realistically, I can't know where I'm going to be, health-wise. There have been doctors who say, 'Just accept it; use a wheelchair.' I'm not willing to do that. I want to retain as much strength as I can for as long as I can.

"But my hope is that this next surgery goes very well, that I regain a lot of strength and stamina. I'd love to put together a comic book that a publisher would pick up. I'm excited about working on more projects with Eros." She chuckles. "And who knows—maybe we'll get a second bunny!" ■

Paul

THREE *F's and two I's.*

My first semester grades hit me like a kick in the stomach. The *F's* were for classes where my work was poor. The *I's* were "incompletes"—for courses in which I never finished my assignments. They eventually became *F's*, too.

I crumpled the report card and shoved it deep in a trashcan. I can't say I was surprised. A zero grade-point average was what I deserved, no question about it. But seeing my name in print on the worst possible report card still hurt. It also lit a spark in me, one that changed my life.

I was nineteen when I bombed out my first year of college. I hadn't always been a poor student. During elementary and middle school, I was consistently at the top of my class. But when I transferred into a huge regional high school, everything changed. I started "underachieving." Guidance counselors, teachers, and members of my family noticed. "You have potential," they'd say when they heard of my mediocre performance. "You just don't apply yourself."

They didn't understand. The truth was I *did* apply myself—just not to academics. As a shy, acne-prone teenager thrown into an enormous and unfamiliar high school, grades were not my priority; survival was. During my freshman year, I was constantly hassled and teased by a group of older guys at my school. They shoved and threatened me on the bus, teased me in the halls, and mocked me during lunchtime. *Nerd. Geek. Loser.* These insults were fired at me like bullets. Sometimes they came with fists. I got scared.

This fear transformed me. Constantly stressed and distracted, I stopped worrying about classes. Too embarrassed to admit to teachers or my family what was happening, I quietly dropped from an A student in 8th grade to a C student just a year later. My definition of success changed just as dramatically. To me, a good day at school was no longer about doing well in class. It was simply about getting home without being hassled. To achieve this goal, I learned to blend into the crowd—to look, talk, and act like the popular kids. First, I changed my clothes and hairstyle. Then I started behaving differently, hanging out with new "friends" and teasing the few kids who fit in worse than me. By the end of my freshman year, I escaped being at the bottom of the social ladder, but I also gave up on being a good student.

Instead, my focus was on following the crowd and being a social success. In 10th grade, I got a job at a nearby mall, so I could buy what seemed important: name-brand clothes, expensive sneakers, the latest CD's, and movie tickets—things I thought I needed to be popular. So what if my grades tumbled because I neglected my studies? At least no one was laughing at me anymore. By 11th grade, a new girlfriend and my used car were what I cared most about. Classes were a meaningless activity I endured weekdays. Senior year was more of the same, though I took the SAT and applied to a few colleges— because classmates were doing it. Despite my mediocre grades, I managed to get accepted.

The following September, thanks to my family's savings, I followed the crowd and floated straight to college.

That's when I started to sink. Years of putting social time and my job ahead of school left me without study habits to deal with college work. Years of coasting in class left me unready for assignments that required effort and time-management skills. Years of following others left me unequipped to make smart choices about my education. In addition to lacking skills, I also lacked motivation. College felt as meaningless to me as high school. Though I'd gotten accepted at a four-year university, nothing pushed me to succeed there. I arrived on campus in September without skills, goals, and a plan. I figured I could continue doing what I had done for years: coasting. It was a recipe for disaster.

My first week on campus, I coasted through freshman orientation, skipping activities because I didn't take them seriously. My second week, I attended a few parties, got home late, and overslept, missing a bunch of classes. No big deal, I thought. I'd just float by and hand in my homework late. But I quickly discovered, unlike high school, catching up was difficult in college. Readings in my English and history classes were longer and more complicated than I was used to—too difficult for me to skim. Writing assignments were more numerous and required more time than I'd expected. Unaccustomed to the workload, I started cutting "easy" classes to complete overdue assignments from other courses. This strategy made me fall farther behind, which, in turn, made it even more difficult to motivate myself to attend class.

Why bother if you're already behind? I thought.

Deadlines passed and work kept piling up, and I began to realize I was in over my head. Halfway through the semester, I stopped going to classes regularly, hoping instead that I could score well on final exams to offset my missing assignments. But without attending class and taking notes, there was no way I could adequately prepare for tests. While coasting worked in high school, it didn't work in college. By the end of ten weeks, I knew I was done. No longer able to float, I'd sunk. My family was stunned and disappointed at my failure. I was, too, though the lesson hadn't yet fully sunk in.

That happened a few months later when I was working at a large warehouse store called Sam's Club—the one place near home that would hire an unskilled college dropout in the middle of winter. My job was to retrieve shopping carts from the store's massive parking lot and stack them in rows for customers. Days and nights, I trudged across the dismal asphalt, collecting carts and cleaning up piles of garbage and soiled diapers shoppers left behind. On this March afternoon, it was raw and stormy, and I was wearing a used yellow Sam's Club raincoat that made me stink of sweat and vinyl. My hair was dripping, and my shoes squished like soaked sponges with each step.

The store was crowded with shoppers, and I'd just shoved a heavy train of carts next to the front door when a cluster of young people walked out. I recognized them immediately: four popular classmates who'd gone to my high school. They were giggling about something—a sound that brought me back to the time, years earlier, when I feared being laughed at by my peers. My face began to burn.

"Oh my God, it's *Paul*," said one of them. They all looked at me. I felt trapped.

"What are *you* doing here?" said Ken, a guy who'd been in my English class in 10th grade. He glanced at my rain-soaked jacket.

"Working," I said. There was an awkward silence. I had spent years trying to fit in with people like them, and now I only wanted to get away. "What about you?" I asked, hoping to change the subject.

"We're home for spring break," Ken replied.

The burning on my face suddenly grew hotter. They were already finishing their first year of college, and I was pushing carts in the rain—pushing carts for them.

"Paul, we need more carts in here! Hurry up!!!" my supervisor yelled from inside the store.

My former classmates looked uncomfortable and embarrassed. I could see the questions in their eyes. *What happened to you? Weren't you in college too?* I felt as if my first-semester grade-point average was written across my face, and they were reading it.

Zero point zero.

I nodded a quick goodbye and turned away. My eyes stung as the truth of my mistakes poured down on me like the rain. I had allowed myself to become what my grade-point average said: a failure—a dropout without a plan, a goal, or a real future. A zero. Coasting wasn't going to carry me any further. Neither would the CD's, the parties, or the brand-name sneakers I'd so valued in high school. By pursuing them and nothing else, I'd closed doors in my life. If I kept following the same path, I could spend years struggling in that dreary parking lot or some other menial job while my peers moved forward. I wanted to do more with my life than push shopping carts.

The spark which ignited at the sight of my report card erupted into a burning flame in my chest. Watching my friends drive off that afternoon, one thing was suddenly clear to me: it was time to get serious and take control of my life. College could help me do that, I realized. It could be a lifeline; I just had to grab it—no more coasting.

The following fall, with money saved from working nine months in the parking lot, I paid for classes at a local community college. This time, I attended every orientation activity—and I took notes. Learning from past mistakes, I also bought a calendar and jotted down each assignment, so I could see deadlines well in advance and plan accordingly. Instead of skipping classes for social time, I arranged social events after class with peers who seemed serious about their work. No longer a follower, I became a study group leader! This actually helped me become a popular student—the thing I had chased for so long in high school.

I am not going to say it was easy. After long days on the job, I spent longer nights at home doing my coursework. It took months of practice for me to learn the skills I'd missed in high school: how to take good notes, how to take tests, how to write an effective essay, and how to get help when I needed it. But gradually I learned.

Throughout my second attempt at college, I sat beside many students who reminded me of myself during my first semester. I recognized them right away—students who seemed distracted or apathetic in class or who were frequently absent. They usually disappeared after a few weeks. Some were dealing with full lives that made it difficult to focus on their courses. Others, especially the ones straight out of high school, were coasting, unsure of why they were there or what they were doing. For these students, college is especially tough.

To thrive in college, you have to want to be there, and you have to be ready to focus on work. Some people aren't ready. They're likely to fail, just as I did. But even failure, as painful as it is, doesn't have to be an ending. It can be a learning experience—one that builds strength and gives direction. It can also serve as a wake-up call that turns a floating student into a serious one. It can even light a spark that sets the stage for future success. Take it from me, a former zero, who graduated from community college with a perfect 4.0 grade point average! ■

Erika

"*ÁNDALE! Apúrate!* Come on, *niños*! We're gonna be late!"

Luisa and Erick Hilario rush out of their room, carrying schoolbooks, a soccer ball, cleats, and water bottles. Their mom, Erika, hurries them out the door and down the narrow steps of their apartment building. She carries a cooler filled with cut-up fruit. They hit the sidewalk almost running.

The Hilarios are in a hurry. That is true on this particular day, when they're starting the two-plus-hour trip by train, bus, and foot from their neighborhood in Los Angeles to Pasadena. There, Luisa, 11, plays with one of the best soccer clubs in California. It is true on every other day as well. On weekends and weekdays, from early mornings to late evenings, in Spanish and in English, the family hurries. On the soccer field, Luisa scores goals. Off the field, the family focuses on goals of another sort—goals that go far beyond the soccer field.

"Through soccer, Luisa sees another world," Erika says. In their own neighborhood, Boyle Heights, most residents have not finished high school. More Spanish is heard than English. Luisa and Erick's father is a long-distance trucker who is rarely home. To earn money, Luisa decorates notebooks with colorful duct tape and sells them to her classmates, and Erick, 8, picks up recyclable bottles and cans. But in Pasadena, where the "CZ Elite" soccer club practices, Luisa plays alongside the children of doctors, lawyers, and professors. Those kids will go on to highly ranked universities. They will have professional careers, live in fancy houses, and be financially independent. These are all things that Erika desperately wants for her own children—especially for Luisa. In Luisa, Erika sees the little girl she once was, and the chances that she never had.

"Life is very heavy for a woman," says Erika. "Women have to be the models if things are going to change." And Erika is determined things *are* going to change. Her brown-skinned children are going to enjoy the same opportunities as the wealthier Anglos around them, even if it takes her last ounce of strength to make it so. Although Erika's own life has indeed been heavy, she has taken her own pain and turned it into something amazingly strong and positive.

From the outside, Erika doesn't seem unusual. She didn't finish high school. She is a pretty woman, but doesn't fuss over her appearance. Her usual uniform is sweat pants and T-shirts. Her beautiful red-brown hair is pulled back into a messy ponytail. She struggles with English, substituting the occasional Spanish word when she forgets. For work, she picks up a little money counting tortillas on a factory assembly line. But as she tells her own story, it becomes clear that she is extraordinary. Thinking back over the years, she can't keep tears from spilling down her cheeks. But she dries those tears and reminds herself, "Like I tell my kids—look forward, always forward. Never back."

Erika was born in Mexico City, 32 years ago, to poor parents who could not read or write. Her father worked as a driver; her mother cleaned houses for rich families. Erika was the middle child of five siblings. As she grew up, she realized that her father had another wife and children elsewhere in town. Nobody seemed to think that was unusual. And no one thought it was unusual that he beat Erika's mother and the children.

"My father was very *machista*," she says, using the Spanish word that means sexist, overbearing, and often abusive to women. "He controlled our home entirely. If my mother went to the market to buy a chicken, he might decide she was with another man. So he'd beat her when she came home. He would hit us for anything, even spilling a drop of water. We lived in a crowded city, but we had no friends. We weren't supposed to even say hello to people. We kids went to school and came home."

Worse yet, when Erika was nine, her father began to sexually abuse her. Erika tried to tell her mother, but it did no good. "In my house, to speak of sex was a sin," she says, tears running down her cheeks. "She never did anything to help me. But I do not blame her. I love my mother. She was ignorant; she was afraid. I can't judge her."

Instead of blaming her mother, Erika tried to help her. "My father would threaten to leave us, and she'd cry and say, 'No, no.' I'd tell her, 'Let him go! We'll be better off!' When he'd hit her, I'd try to pull him off."

Erika's strong spirit made her father angry. When she finished elementary school, he told her he would no longer pay her school fees. "I loved school," she says. "I threw myself at his feet, begging him to let me study. But he said that educating a girl was throwing money away."

And so, at the age of 11—the age Luisa is today—Erika went to work. She attended school in the morning, took the bus home, showered, and put on a work uniform. By 3 o'clock she was at a local market, where she and other children bagged groceries and stocked shelves for tips. By working until midnight, she was able to keep paying her school fees for three more years.

When Erika was 14, she began seeing a boy who was four years older. As her boyfriend, he was "sweet, nice. Never jealous." He taught her some valuable skills—how to drive a car, how to change a tire. She ran away from home to live with him, to get away from her abusive father.

But once Erika moved in with the boyfriend, everything changed. Now he began to act like her father—*machista*. He hit her if she so much as said "good morning" to another man. In addition, he used drugs, which he introduced Erika to.

Finally a crisis came. Erika was asleep when her boyfriend, crazy on drugs, attacked her with his fists, beating her savagely. "I truly thought I was going to die," she remembers. In great pain, blood streaming down her face, she ran from one neighbor's apartment to another, begging for help. (She learned later she had a fractured skull.) One after another, women turned her away. "They said they didn't want a problem," Erica says bitterly. They were too afraid of their husbands to help a beaten woman.

Afraid to stay in the same town with her ex-boyfriend, Erika fled to another part of Mexico to live with an uncle's family. There she thought about her options. Ahead of her, she could see two ways of life. "I could live like my mother. Or I could be with bad people, the drugs and all that. I said no, those are not for me."

Erika spoke to another uncle, one who was living in Los Angeles. He offered to help her come to the United States.

"He would pay a *coyote* (a person hired to smuggle people) to take me across the border," she says. "I decided to go. I would live in L.A., pay him back, and start a new life."

Erika's first attempt to cross the border almost ended any hopes she had of a better life— or perhaps of life at all.

She was one of a group of 50 people, 49 of whom were men. They were guided by three *coyotes*. The group walked for two full days, through desolate desert territory. One *coyote* attached himself to Erika, never leaving her side. As the group became more scattered, he separated her from the others.

"I didn't know where I was," Erika says. "We lost sight of the group, and I was alone with him. He began saying dirty things." She was terrified, but there was nowhere to go to get away. Finally they stopped to rest, sheltering under a rock. The *coyote* became aggressive. He tried to force Erika to touch him in sexual ways. She fought him off, moving as far from him as she could. Finally he fell asleep.

Alone in the desert night, Erika wept with rage and fear. She thought of her father's abuse, of her boyfriend's beatings. "I thought, 'WHY? Why me, again? Why do men treat women like this, like *basura*, like garbage? We are not objects just to be used!'"

Looking at the sleeping man, she thought of what he would do when he woke. She came to a decision. "I will not let this happen," she told herself. "If I have to kill him, I will do it." She searched for a heavy rock. She held it, thinking how she would smash his head.

And then the Border Patrol showed up.

"Thank God they came," Erika says, shaking her head at the horror of the memory. "I would have assassinated him."

Erika and the rest of the group were taken back into Mexico, where they were held briefly in jail and then released. After a week, Erika was ready to try again. Again, she traveled with a group of 50 people, but this time the *coyote* "was a good person. He told us, 'If you have food, share it.' When it snowed, he covered me with his *chamarra*, his jacket."

Soon, Erika reached Los Angeles. In time, she gained legal residency in the U.S. She met her husband, Luis, a gentle man 11 years older than she. As Luisa and then Erick came along, Erika discovered a passion for parenting. She threw herself into learning English. "In Mexico, we have a saying, *'A la tierra que fueres, haz lo que vieres.'* When you go to a new place, you do as those people do. And to help my children here, I have to speak English."

As the children started school, Erika became determined that though they were not rich, and were the children of immigrants, and didn't live in a fancy part of town, they were still going to get opportunities that more privileged American kids get. When classmates at Luisa's kindergarten teased her about her crooked teeth, making her self-conscious about smiling, Erika pulled her out. She went to a local private school and begged until they gave her a discount on tuition. She enrolled Luisa (and later Erick), cut her household budget to the bone, and somehow found the money every month to pay the fees.

Erika watched her children's school progress like a hawk, demanding that they do their best. She posted learning tools, like multiplication tables and spelling lists, all over the house. She refused to install cable TV. "We can use that money for shoes and for lessons," she said. She went to library sales to buy inexpensive books to fill the bookcase that stands in Erick and Luisa's bedroom.

Today, all of Erika's efforts are paying off. The children are excellent students. Luisa is preparing to take the admission test to one of the highest-ranked middle schools in Los Angeles. "We will have to work very, very hard," says Erika. When Erika speaks of her children's futures, she always says, "We." Recently, the family was written about in a story in the *Los Angeles Times*. To everyone's delight, a reader offered to pay for Luisa to get her teeth straightened. She now proudly flashes a mouth full of braces. Friendly and giggly, she mentions that she dreams of being a professional soccer player.

Erika reminds her, "Maybe, but not many people can play professional soccer. You need Plan B."

Luisa agrees. "I'd also like to be a veterinarian," she says. Erika nods in approval. That is a more realistic goal.

Thanks to her mother, Luisa knows that her dreams can become a reality. She can go to college. She can become a veterinarian, or a professional athlete. She lives in a world where women are not treated like *basura*.

"Luisa sees her teammates, and their families," her mom says. "I tell her, she can study and work, and she can live like them. She can be independent, not having to rely on anyone else. Or, she can stay in this house and be one of those." Erika points to the alley beside the house, where young people hang out to smoke marijuana.

"I don't judge them," she says of the pot smokers. "I was one of them. But my children— they deserve more."

Erika sends her children off to complete their homework. She'll check it when they are done. Later in the evening, she'll bring a whiteboard into the living room, where Luisa's soccer ribbons and trophies line a shelf, so they can have a Spanish lesson. Erika insists that the children be fully bilingual, using perfect grammar in both languages.

As the children study, and Erika cleans up the kitchen from dinner, her words hang in the air: "Women have to be the models if things are going to change." Once beaten, abused, and denied an education, the amazing Erika Hilario has found the strength to become that model. ■

Jeroboam

THE famous children's story "The Ugly Duckling" begins something like this:

A mother duck is sitting on a nest of eggs. When the eggs hatch, there are several ordinary-looking ducklings and one big, strange-looking chick. "What an ugly duckling," everyone says. The other birds peck at him and drive him away. "You're different. You're ugly. We don't want you around," they tell him.

Jeroboam Bozeman knows how the little duckling felt.

As a kid growing up in Brooklyn, he wasn't ugly. But he was different. He liked jumping Double Dutch with the girls better than playing football with the boys. He preferred laughing and playing to fighting. As a result, he was picked on and bullied. Other boys beat him up and called him ugly names.

Fortunately, unlike the ugly duckling, Jeroboam had a supportive family. His mom and dad loved him. One of seven children, he has a fraternal (not identical) twin named Jehoshaphat. When boys threatened to beat Jeroboam up, his twin would step in and say, "You want to fight someone? Fight me."

Besides his family, he had another love: dancing. He's been dancing as long as he can remember.

"I'd wake up early and turn on MTV or BET," he recalls. "I'd watch Michael Jackson and Britney Spears and NSYNC, and I'd try to imitate what I saw. I'd get my girl friends together and teach them dances that we did at block parties, as the boys didn't want to dance."

When his mother saw Jeroboam's love for dance, she enrolled him at the Ronald Edmonds Learning Center, a middle school that specializes in arts education. His dance teacher, Ruth Sistaire, was the first of many dance mentors in his life. "Ms. Sistaire was an amazing teacher," he says. "She was a little tiny lady who was very stern but loving. She taught me well!"

Dance became the most important thing in Jeroboam's life. African dance, hip-hop, classical dance—they were places he could escape to, in his mind at least, from a world where he felt out of step. His passion became stronger when one of his teachers took him to see a performance by the Alvin Ailey American Dance Theater. The Ailey group is a world-famous modern dance company. Founded in 1958, it was for years made up of predominantly Black performers. (Most of its dancers are still African American.)

For Jeroboam, a young Black boy who danced even in his dreams, seeing the Ailey group perform was a life-changing experience. "To see these wonderful dancers who looked like *me*—that was just amazing."

The evening included a strange incident. At intermission, Jeroboam went into the restroom and noticed a man he thought he recognized. When he returned to his group, Jeroboam excitedly told his teacher, "I saw Mr. Ailey! He smiled at me!"

His teacher told him, "That's not possible—Mr. Ailey passed away."

But the memory stuck with Jeroboam. From that evening on, he wanted to be an Ailey dancer. He worked harder than ever, training at the Creative Outlet Dance Theatre of Brooklyn. He began to believe that he was truly talented—that maybe being a professional dancer could become a reality.

Then trouble struck, trouble that threatened to destroy Jeroboam's dreams.

The Bozeman family fell on hard times. To Jeroboam, it seemed to happen overnight.

"I was about 13," Jeroboam remembers. "Maybe my older siblings understood what was going on, but I didn't. All I knew is that we were cleaning the house like crazy. I thought it was just for the fun of it. But I realize now we were preparing to leave. Late one night, my mom said, 'We have to go.' We packed our van, put some things in storage, and left."

The family's destination was a homeless shelter in the Bronx. Jeroboam had to leave his school—and his dance lessons.

"The first night, I wouldn't go into the shelter," Jeroboam says. "I lay in the van, crying my eyes out." When his dance teacher heard what had happened, she offered to let Jeroboam live with her family. But Jeroboam's mother refused.

"Whatever happens," she said, "my family stays together."

After a few weeks, the family (Mom, Dad, and five kids—the two oldest had moved out by then) was transferred to a shelter back in Brooklyn, where they stayed for the next three years. It was a grim atmosphere. "The seven of us had three bedrooms—very tight quarters. There were shootings in the street almost daily. Our parents did all they could to protect us. We weren't allowed to go outside. My mom's constant refrain was, 'I am not going to lose my babies to the street.'"

During those years, Jeroboam saw what his mother was worried about. Friends and schoolmates were drifting into street life. He saw smart, talented young people lost to drugs, to violence, to crime.

The bullying continued. Without dance in his life, Jeroboam began to slip into despair. He felt alone, misunderstood, and unheard. After a particularly brutal attack, he stopped speaking regularly. For two years he was "selectively mute," meaning that he spoke only in certain situations. "I told myself, no one listens to me anyway, so why should I talk?" At school, he communicated in sign language or by writing notes. At home, he spoke freely when he needed to.

Fortunately, the ugly duckling's spirit did not die. And once the family was out of the shelter and back in its own apartment, Jeroboam found his way back to the Creative Outlet Dance Theatre. He threw himself back into dance with renewed passion. Just after he graduated high school, an incredible opportunity came his way. The Broadway musical *Aida*, with music by Elton John, was touring China. A friend of Jeroboam's was in the show. When another dancer had to take an emergency leave from the tour, the friend recommended Jeroboam. He did well at a private audition. His interviewer asked, "Can you be ready in a few days?" Somehow, he was. He spent three months in China, dancing in the show.

The time he spent with *Aida* added to Jeroboam's reputation as an up-and-coming talent. He moved from New York to Philadelphia, where he joined Philadanco, the Philadelphia Dance Company. He was only 19 years old, still very much a kid. Artistic Director Joan Myers Brown, his boss, gave him the tools to be a professional.

"I loved being with Philadanco," he recalls. "But learning the skills needed for a dance career at that caliber was intense. Everything hurt. I was a HUGE complainer, always whining, even crying.

"And Ms. Brown had a conversation with me. She looked me in the eye and said, 'You are a talented dancer, but you can't be successful complaining. You're tall, and you will be lifting girls most of your career.'"

Jeroboam took her words to heart. He realized that talent wasn't going to be enough—he was going to have to work harder than he ever had in his life.

"I hit the gym," he remembers. "I started going to rehearsal early, before anyone else—I mean, I'd show up with the janitors. I'd stretch, I'd work out. I was not going to fail."

Ms. Brown's lessons extended beyond dancing.

"She had high, HIGH expectations of us," Jeroboam recalls. "For instance, when we'd go on tour, she'd remind us, 'You are representing Philadanco every moment of the day. When you show up at the airport, you will dress well. You will carry yourself well. You will speak well.' I wanted to show up in pajamas, which wasn't a good representation. But she was right. She taught me to be a professional."

Eventually Jeroboam felt ready to audition for his dream employer—the Alvin Ailey company.

He didn't make it.

He auditioned again. And again. And again. He still didn't make it.

Finally, when he was 22, he was offered a place in Ailey II, the company's second group.

At the time, he was working with the Spectrum Dance Theater in Seattle, Washington. Spectrum is a dance company with a fine reputation. To join Ailey II would mean a loss of pay, as well as a loss of status. Some of his friends thought he was crazy to give up his good job in Seattle.

Jeroboam didn't hesitate. He joined Ailey II.

"I knew—I KNEW—if I could just get my foot in the door, I would someday get into the first company."

He threw himself into working with Ailey II, even though he didn't intend to stay there.

"At one point, someone saw me packing my bag to take my dance clothes home. He said, 'You know, there are lockers here you can use.' I said, 'No thanks; I don't intend to be here that long.'"

A year passed.

Ailey II had just come back from a tour. They were performing in New York City for two weeks. The day after, they were leaving for a tour in Italy.

Jeroboam was exhausted.

But there was an audition for Ailey—the first company.

As tired as he was, Jeroboam went.

"I figured I had nothing to lose," he said. "I danced like a madman. And at the end, out of more than 100 male dancers who auditioned, I was the only one who was hired."

When he got the news, Jeroboam burst out laughing.

"I literally couldn't believe it," he says.

It was only late that night that the truth hit him.

"I had moved back home," he says. "On the Ailey II salary, I couldn't afford my own place. So I was lying in my old bed and I said out loud to the ceiling, 'It's happening. You did it.'"

As he tells the story, tears begin to run down Jeroboam's face.

"It was . . . such a relief," he says, through his sobs. "To have heard all those years, 'You're not good enough. You don't have what it takes. You're a poor kid from Brooklyn. Maybe you should look into working retail.'

"After all those years training, rehearsing in studios, looking at the Ailey posters on the walls, touring, and to finally hear the YES . . ."

To hear the "yes." To be part of a group he had always dreamed of.

That was in 2013. In the brief time he has been part of the Ailey company, Jeroboam Bozeman has become a star. On Christmas Day 2015, the *New York Times* published a profile of Jeroboam on the front page of its Arts section. It talked about how Jeroboam, now 25, was having a "breakout season" with the company, praising his "rugged grace" and noting that he has "triumphed in lead roles."

The article also talked about Jeroboam's difficult years—the homelessness, the bullying, the years of silence. Those details were a surprise to his coworkers and even many of his friends.

"I've never wanted to be seen as that poor, pitiful boy from Brooklyn," he explained. "So I didn't talk about the hard times. But I've realized—it's time to let it go. No more secrets. You can't move on while you're holding onto negative things."

Most importantly, he wants to share his story, the bad as well as the good, with the other ugly ducklings of the world.

"I want kids to know how talented and beautiful and important they are," he says. "I was healed through dance. I want, more than anything, to help kids find the means to heal themselves."

This is how the story "The Ugly Duckling" ends:

The duckling, rejected by everyone, spends a long lonely winter by a pond. When spring comes, he sees a flock of beautiful swans swim into view. He thinks they are coming to attack him. Instead, they surround and welcome him lovingly. He bows his head and sees his reflection in the water. He, the ugly duckling, has grown into the most beautiful swan of them all. ■

Tay Thi

TAY THI Nguyen is one of the mightiest people I've met, at 94 pounds. She has a towering presence, at a bit more than 5 feet tall. She is so strong that she probably could bench press 25 pounds.

Three times Tay Thi has fainted while here at college, training to become an English teacher, because she starved herself to afford tuition. But she had the strength to persist and soon will become the first person in her village to graduate from college, and she embodies such grit and selflessness that, to me, she's the world's college graduate of the year.

Tay Thi, 20, also underscores the principle—especially important in the aftermath of the kidnapping of the Nigerian schoolgirls—that the best leverage we have to achieve social change is to educate girls.

The eighth of nine children born into an impoverished farming family in the Mekong Delta, Tay Thi shone in school, but her mother demanded—unsuccessfully—that she drop out after primary school and earn money as a live-in housemaid in distant Ho Chi Minh City.

"She got very angry with me," Tay Thi recalled. In eighth grade, her mom burned her school books to try to force her to drop out, but Tay Thi borrowed books and continued to excel.

Staying in school was possible because of the help she received from Room to Read, an aid group that sponsored Tay Thi and covered her school fees, uniform, books, bicycle to get to school, and other expenses.

Tay Thi persevered, even when her parents again burned her books in 12th grade, and, as she graduated from high school, she prepared secretly for the college entrance examination. Her mother found out about this when Tay Thi left to take the exam and lashed out, saying, "I hope you fail the exams."

Other students arrived at the exam location escorted by cheering, doting parents; Tay Thi arrived alone, sobbing. Still, she aced the exam.

With no parental subsidy, college seemed unaffordable, but Tay Thi saved every penny she could. She had long worked every vacation—sometimes in a factory job by day and in a duck soup restaurant by night until 2 a.m. Even during Vietnamese New Year celebrations, she worked in the fields by herself to catch crabs for money—watching the fireworks in the distance.

At college, Tay Thi confined herself to a food budget of $3.50—*per week*. Malnourished, she sometimes toppled over in the middle of class in a dead faint.

Professors and students discovered that she was starved and basically penniless—leaving Tay Thi feeling humiliated. "I was so upset about that," she said, but, in retrospect, it was a turning point because her teachers and classmates responded with kindness, sympathy and help.

Room to Read arranged a corporate scholarship, which gave her a bit more spending money, and Tay Thi managed to eat enough to keep from fainting in public.

Tay Thi shares a small room with two other young women, all sleeping on the floor next to each other. She set up a small reading light that won't keep the others awake. She studies until midnight, and then sets her alarm for 4 a.m. to resume studying.

She is just as passionate about education for others. First, she encouraged her older brother to return to school, after years of working as a laborer, so he could become a mechanic. When he resisted, Tay Thi went out and registered him as a student, picking his courses and browbeating him until he gave in.

Then she coaxed her younger brother to follow her to college, where he is now a freshman. Even her parents have come around, partly because they see that Tay Thi will soon be an English teacher—and the best-paid member of the extended family.

Tay Thi is trying to arrange to teach in her own remote village school, where she wants to advocate for education. "I would like to change people's thinking," she says. "It's a way of helping children in my community," she said.

The kidnappings in Nigeria have put a spotlight on girls' education, and Tay Thi is an example of why the issue is critical. It's sometimes said that if you send a boy to school, you educate a man; if you send a girl to school, you educate a village. That's not always true, but empowering girls remains one of the best ways to empower a community. Girls' education also strongly correlates to reduced family size. When I asked Tay Thi if she planned to have nine children like her mom, she roared with laughter and gave a firm "NO!"

So let's celebrate the mightiest college graduate of this commencement season, a young woman of incomparable strength who now is thrilled at the prospect of returning to an impoverished farming village to teach children and change the world. ■

Indonesia
and Ericka

WHEN she was a single, pregnant teen in Camden, New Jersey, Ericka Young knew what the statistics said about the baby she was going to have. It wasn't a pretty picture.

She knew that babies born to teens have the deck stacked against them. Especially in poor urban areas, they are at risk for abuse and neglect. The boys are more likely than other children to end up in prison; the girls are more likely to get pregnant as teens. Many do not complete high school. Few of them go on to college.

But even at the age of 15, Ericka had other plans for her child. She named the little girl Indonesia. She chose the unusual name, she told people, "because this girl is going places."

Between them, Ericka and Indonesia Young have made that prediction come true. In 2015, Indonesia graduated with honors from Camden Catholic High School. Her high-school transcript is stuffed with accomplishments, including advanced placement and honors courses, high SAT scores, and participation in the Rutgers University law school "moot court" (a competition where high-school students argue a made-up law case). She's been a strong presence in her community, volunteering with the Salvation Army, at her former elementary school, and at the local soup kitchen, where she cooks and plates foods for people who stop in for a free lunch. Her writing has been published in the *Philadelphia Inquirer*. She's an enthusiastic reader and a fan of old black and white movies, and she loves hip-hop. She dreams of visiting Spain and of teaching in Africa. And now she is headed to Temple University in Philadelphia, the recipient of a full-ride scholarship.

Not bad for a daughter of a teen mom in Camden.

How did Indo beat the odds, and beat them so thoroughly?

It had a lot to do with her mother's refusal to settle for what she saw around her.

When Indo was born, Ericka was living with her extended family in her grandmother's house. As many as 20 people from four generations crowded under that roof. Those included Ericka's mom, who had had two children by the time she was 14. There were other babies and children there—cousins who, Ericka could see, weren't being parented right. Ericka's own older brothers had children they didn't care for. Her mother, having had children at such a young age, hadn't ever really grown up. "Other people always took care of her," Ericka remembers. "She felt entitled. She never really stepped into the role of being a mom."

It wasn't a terrible place. There was always a roof over their heads and food on the table.

But it wasn't a good place, either. There was little structure. People came and went. Relatives, including Ericka's brothers, were in and out of jail. No one had a steady job. Worst of all, from Ericka's point of view, there were no hugs and kisses, no snuggling, no playful attention. "My mom and grandma weren't cold, exactly, but they didn't show affection," Ericka remembers.

"I wanted a mom who would hug me and tell me she loved me. I determined I was going to show my child a lot of love."

But if she knew how she *didn't* want to live, Ericka needed role models to show her what she *did* want. She found them on TV—on situation comedies like *The Cosby Show* and *Diff'rent Strokes.*

"People say bad things about Bill Cosby now, but I didn't know any of that," she says today. "What I saw was a perfect family. They were educated—he was a doctor, she was a lawyer. They were affectionate and had fun with their kids. They cared how the kids did in school. In *Diff'rent Strokes*, I saw Arnold and Willis living in this nice house in a nice neighborhood. I saw all that, and I wanted it."

Determined to provide a different kind of life for Indonesia, Ericka returned to high school soon after her baby was born. After graduating, she took community college classes on and off for three years, studying legal secretary work and medical assistant work. She took jobs—jobs she didn't necessarily like, but jobs that allowed her to support herself and Indo. As soon as she could afford it, she got her own house. "Indo has had her own room since she was 3," Ericka says proudly. "We've got our own peaceful place, where we can sit all day and nobody bothers us. Not like my growing up with dozens of people around."

And from the beginning, she thought about the example she was setting for her daughter. "Living on public assistance isn't for me," she says firmly. "We pay our way." She gestures to the street that runs outside their house. "You see those young men out there, skating up and down the street? That's how they spend their days." She looks proudly at her daughter. "Indonesia doesn't have time for that. She's too busy studying or working."

And truly, Indo has been busy from an early age. Before she began preschool, Ericka enrolled her in a six-week program called Junior Explorers. There, Indonesia learned to write her name and got used to the idea of school. "She loved it!" Ericka remembers. "And she learned that school was a happy place to be."

When Indo was older, Ericka signed her up for Girl Scouts. By then, Ericka had been trained in CPR (cardiopulmonary resuscitation, a lifesaving technique) and first aid. When the Girl Scouts were earning their own First Aid badges, Ericka was their instructor.

Indonesia went to public school until she started fifth grade. Then her mom, concerned that she wasn't getting the best education, transferred her to Sacred Heart, a Catholic school in the heart of Camden.

The move was a shock to Indonesia in several ways. "My elementary school was a block from my house. Sacred Heart was further away, in a really suffering area. It's not a place where kids can play outside. We'd find needles on the playground. And we aren't religious, so the prayers and Catholic stuff were an adjustment." But she enjoyed being at a school where teachers had high expectations of her.

As she moved into high school at Camden Catholic, the academic pressures increased. "I was in class with kids who were better prepared than I was," she remembers. "Their parents were college graduates. I had to work really hard to get into my AP and Honors classes."

There was a financial gap between Indo and her classmates as well. A number were from families who were better off than hers. While she worked at Wal-Mart for two years in order to buy a used car for $650, some of her classmates received brand new cars as graduation gifts. It seemed that everyone had the latest version iPhone and iPad, while Indo didn't even have a cell phone.

There were days that those things bothered her, but today, Indo shrugs them off. "I noticed that for the most part, the students with the most money had the lowest goals. They weren't in the top honors or AP courses. They didn't work for high SAT scores. They just counted on their families paying for them to attend whatever college they wished."

Meanwhile, Indo says, "I watched my mother struggle at jobs she hated. I saw classmates blow the price of my car on prom dresses. I learned that nobody owed me anything, and that it was up to me to become an accomplished individual. So I pushed myself hard to get into the top classes, even when it seemed insane to other people."

Some people did think Indo was crazy for working so hard. She felt the distance growing between her and some of her childhood friends and relatives. "They'd laugh at me, tell me I was a nerd, that I wasn't cool," she remembers. "Most of my cousins have that street mentality."

Ericka came in for criticism as well. Some friends told her, "Are you crazy, sending your child to a Catholic school when you could send her to public school for free?"

Others would talk disapprovingly about Indonesia. "She talks like a white girl," they'd say. Ericka was having none of that. "She talks properly," she'd fire back. "You're the one who doesn't know how to talk right."

And there have been times Ericka has been lonely, feeling out of step with many of her peers. While Indonesia is going off to college, Ericka is only 34.

"A lot of girls my age, they don't get me," she says. "I've heard, 'Oh, she thinks she knows it all. She's uppity. She thinks she's better than other people.'"

While such comments might sting, Ericka hasn't let them get her down.

"The fact is, I *do* feel better than them," she says. "I've done well. I've got a portfolio of education that can't be taken away from me. I'm proud that I've completed what I started."

Like her mother, Indonesia took education very seriously. When it came time to apply to college, she chose nine: all three Rutgers University branches (in Newark, Camden, and New Brunswick, New Jersey); Spelman College, a historically Black college for women in Atlanta, Georgia; Penn State; Seton Hall in New Jersey; Rowan University, also in New Jersey; the College of New Jersey; and Temple University in Philadelphia. All nine colleges accepted her.

Of all the schools, Temple offered Indonesia the least financial aid. But of all the schools, it was her top choice. Together, Indonesia and her mom decided that, no matter what, Indonesia was going to attend Temple. They reasoned that it was an excellent school; it was reasonably close to home; and it would put Indonesia in touch with many people who could be influential in her future. Both mom and daughter believe in the old saying, "It's not what you know; it's who you know." So if Indonesia had to borrow money to attend Temple, they agreed it would pay off in the end.

That was before Indonesia got the letter.

Dear Indonesia:

It is my pleasure to congratulate you on being awarded the first-ever Lewis Katz Scholarship. This scholarship covers tuition, board, mandatory fees and books for four years at Temple University. . . . This prestigious award is named in memory of beloved Temple University Trustee Lewis Katz, who passed away in a plane crash in May of 2014.

"Lewis Katz was born and raised in Camden, New Jersey. His mother had two jobs, and raised her two children on her own after his father died when Lewis was one year old. He was given a scholarship to go to Temple University, and this shaped his life immeasurably. At Temple's 2014 commencement, where Lewis Katz was the featured speaker, he said, 'Some unknown person made the decision to open that door and give that scholarship to a kid from Camden. . . .'"

Indonesia Young is a kid from Camden. And as Ericka predicted at her birth—she's going places. As she goes, she'll be taking along the lessons taught her by her wise and determined mother. ∎

Peter

WHEN Peter Travis found himself homeless again, he fell into depression and thoughts of suicide. He'd been homeless as a boy, sleeping in a tent with his mother and father outside of Kingston, New York, while cold winds rattled the tent walls. Now he was on the streets again, but this time those streets were in Reno, Nevada, where the homeless shelter was little more than a warehouse, a place to keep people like him out of sight of tourists in the gambling casinos. And this time he had a wife, a child, and, he's quick to add, a dog named Shamrock.

The move to Reno had seemed like a good idea at first, given the downturn in Peter's health. He had been a very good mechanic, first in New York and then in Birmingham, Alabama. But then he fell victim to a severe case of fibromyalgia, a disease that made his joints stiff and sore, accompanied by terrible headaches.

"I was so weak and in pain I couldn't turn a wrench anymore," he says.

Worse yet, the headaches led to seizures, as many as fifteen a month, when he would go into a state like sleepwalking, losing awareness of what he was doing or what was being said to him.

Jobless and in constant pain but still determined to improve his life, Peter found the energy to go back to school and get an associate's degree in computer electronics. Then, after research told him that Reno was a city that welcomed workers in this field, he moved his family there, soon finding a job repairing computers for a company called National Cash Register.

But bad luck seemed to follow Peter Travis. The economy took a nosedive, and he was laid off. The fibromyalgia and headaches got worse.

Before long, he was taking massive doses of pain medication that left him in a stupor most of the time. The constant threat of seizures made going to a job interview next to impossible.

Then a bright and unexpected light entered his life, a "gift from God," Peter says. His wife Jaimee suggested they get a puppy to help him deal with his depression and keep him and their new son Erin company. Peter resisted the idea at first—why add another mouth to feed? But when he laid eyes on the dog, a short-haired girl the color of cocoa and whipped cream, he wrapped her up in his jacket and never let go. They named the puppy Shamrock, and the bond she and Peter established was immediate and strong.

Maybe it was Shamrock's herding instinct— she was part Australian cattle dog—or maybe it was that quality some dogs have that allows them to sense a coming earthquake or smell cancer in their owners' bodies, but early on, the pup knew when Peter was going into a seizure. Normally polite and quiet, Shamrock would leap onto Peter's lap and bark, or nip at his hand, or force him to walk in circles until he came out of the daze caused by the seizure. She became his constant companion, and, as luck would have it one day, helped him come out of a seizure that occurred during a doctor's visit. When the doctor witnessed Shamrock's behavior, he wrote a prescription that officially named her a service dog.

"Not bad for a mutt from the Reno dog pound," Peter laughs.

Life was better with Shamrock, but Peter still needed to find work. When he'd go for an interview at a casino, he wouldn't get called back. Before long the interviews dried up altogether, partly, Peter thinks, because word gets around in the casino industry. *Don't call that guy in . . . he brings a dog with him.*

Things hit bottom for him one day when Jaimee was gone and Peter, groggy from pain pills, was taking a nap with two-year-old Erin. Though Jaimee had locked the door to their apartment, Erin still managed to open it and go outside. Fortunately Shamrock followed, because soon the boy walked into traffic while the dog tried to herd him back to safety. Peter woke to police pounding on his door, and even after he'd shown them his medicine bottles, even after he'd convinced them that he wasn't drunk or stoned, he was arrested and charged with child endangerment. He was sentenced to community service, and before long he and Jaimee lost the apartment.

Jaimee had acquaintances in South Bend, Indiana, and, because Child Protective Services didn't allow her to leave Erin alone with Peter, she took Erin and moved to Indiana to try to find work. Peter promised to follow after he'd served out his sentence, but until then he was alone in the Reno homeless shelter, where fistfights and theft were common, where he had only Shamrock for company.

"I didn't think things could get much worse," he says. "I thought about suicide all the time. I might have done it if not for my family and that little dog."

But things could get worse, and they did. When Peter was finally able to join Jaimee in South Bend, she had lost her living arrangements, and the family spent Erin's third birthday on the streets. Soon Jaimee again found a room for her and their son, but Peter spent more nights sleeping on benches or behind gas stations or in church doorways, Shamrock huddled against him to keep them both warm.

Finally, their steps took them to South Bend's Center for the Homeless, a nationally respected program with ties to the University of Notre Dame. Though they didn't know it at first, their lives had entered a new and decidedly different chapter.

"Here we were," Jaimee says, "homeless again. I was no longer prideful, but I felt defeated and heartbroken." But South Bend's center was different from the shelter they'd experienced in Reno. Lectures and counseling filled their days, Erin and Jaimee had a room of their own in the family dorm, programs like "Starting Over/ Stepping Higher" helped them make goals and manage their stress. Slowly things began to change for them, both inside and out.

"I found myself saying, 'Okay, you're homeless,'" Jaimee said, "'but you have a roof over your head, you have food to eat, you have a bed to sleep in. Pull yourself together.'"

Though Peter couldn't stay with Jaimee and Erin in the family dorm, he began to re-examine his life and the choices he'd made. Instead of feeling ashamed of being homeless, he thought of his time at the center as a chance to "catch his breath." His thoughts turned to something his father Wayne had said back in New York. Though the family had struggled there as well, Wayne Travis had never given up, often saying, "If you can't do it one way, find another."

Peter remembered Wayne lifting himself up in his darkest time and finding work at an apartment complex as manager and maintenance supervisor. He remembered a mechanic business where cars would line the lane to his father's shop. He remembered Wayne urging his mother, even during the nights they spent homeless in a tent, to "have faith." Things would work out.

At the same time Peter was re-thinking his life, a near-miracle was happening with his health. While doctors in Reno had been content to numb him with drugs so he could barely function, a doctor in South Bend found the right mix of medicines. Peter's fibromyalgia pain lessened, his headaches became less frequent, and his seizures all but disappeared.

Soon he was searching the Internet for work. And then another miracle: he found a job at Lowe's Home Improvement that allowed—in fact, *welcomed*—a service dog. Soon after, he began substitute teaching at local schools, and the schools welcomed Shamrock as well!

If you can't do it one way, find another.

In time Peter, Jaimee, Erin and Shamrock were able to move into an apartment paid for by the Center for the Homeless. Then an insurance settlement from an accident allowed them to put a down payment on a house, where today Shamrock shares space with a cat named Zoe and a rabbit named Mr. Wiggles.

Peter continues to work at Lowe's (where, like him, Shamrock wears a red Lowe's vest) and substitute teach, while Jaimee pursues her associate's degree in photography, and Erin, a curly-haired five-year-old with boundless energy, attends pre-school at the Center. The insurance payment also allowed Peter to buy tools for a woodshop in the garage, and he plans to return to an old hobby: "rescuing" discarded furniture off the streets and fixing it up for sale at flea markets.

Their new home is, as one would expect, a mess right now, though they've discovered hardwood beneath the worn carpet and are looking forward to renting a sander and making the floor shine.

The other day Jaimee was on her knees in the kitchen, scraping up old linoleum tile and not especially enjoying herself, when she was surprised to feel tears streaming down her face. "I realized," she laughed, "that I would never want to do this for a living, but I thought, *Look at us, we're making a home!*"

Peter, as well, feels overwhelming gratitude for the changes in their lives. "I can't describe the feeling, going from sleeping on the street with Shamrock wrapped in my coat so we could both keep warm, and now with a home of our own." He looks forward to spring so they can plant a vegetable garden, donating a large portion of their harvest to the Center for the Homeless.

Why didn't they give up? Why didn't people in South Bend see them standing on the corner with a cardboard sign? Peter credits his father, Wayne, again, a man who always looked for light in the darkness, who always believed in finding a way. He also points to people at the center who believed in him, and to his boss at Lowe's, who held his job open for months when the accident left him unable to work.

"When we needed it most, we got a hand up, not a handout," he says. He looks toward Shamrock, who is trying to force Zoe the cat from beneath a sofa. "Shamrock, leave the cat alone!" he shouts, and the dog sits up and stares at him, ears forward, eager for whatever comes next. ■

Melissa

IN 2014, nothing was going right for Melissa Alford.

A health crisis had put the 47-year-old in the hospital. As a result, she lost her job, her apartment, and her car. Living in Camden, New Jersey, with her family far away in Georgia, she had nowhere to go. She landed in a homeless shelter.

Such a string of bad luck would make many people throw up their hands in despair. They'd give up, cursing their bad fortune and saying the world was against them.

That's not what Melissa did.

Today, Melissa works full-time (and often more) as a certified nursing assistant (CNA). She's off public assistance. She has her own apartment and is making payments on a car. And she received an award for overcoming her obstacles in record time.

Melissa had come to New Jersey in 2008 to get away from an abusive boyfriend. Like many abusers, he seemed sweet and kind at first. Then he began presenting Melissa with a list of "rules" she was supposed to live by. "No shorts, even on the hottest days," she recalls. "No sleeveless shirts. I wasn't supposed to talk to anybody without his permission. He didn't want me seeing even my own family." His behavior got more unpredictable. "You never knew what was going to make him snap," she says. "He'd walk into a grocery store and think someone was looking at him wrong. That would be enough." Finally, he threatened to beat up Melissa's 25-year-old son, who was born with dwarfism. "That was the last straw," she said.

Melissa packed up and headed north to Camden, where she lived briefly with a cousin. She had worked for years as a CNA in Georgia, and had expected to do the same in New Jersey. But she found that her Georgia certification wasn't accepted in her new state. She quickly got a job at McDonald's, and in four months promoted to assistant manager. She stayed at the job for five years.

But one day, after backing out of her driveway, a terrifying thing happened. Melissa's vision became so blurry she could barely see the road in front of her. Trying not to panic, she crept along the street, with impatient drivers honking their horns behind her. "I kept thinking, 'I just have to keep turning right, and I'll get back to my house,'" she remembers. Fortunately, she managed to get safely home. When she saw a doctor, she learned that she had diabetes that was out of control. Her blood sugar was so high she was in danger of going into a coma.

In the hospital, doctors were able to help Melissa. But by the time she was well enough to work again, she'd lost her job. With no money and no family in the area, she had to go to a shelter—something she'd never imagined doing.

The main reason she'd never thought of being in a shelter is that she'd always worked and paid her own way. But another is that Melissa is a self-described "clean freak." "I can't stand a nasty place!" she says. She laughs as she describes her behavior in the shelter. "Sharing a bathroom with strangers—Lord, no!" she says. "I carried a bottle of bleach around with me. I bought my own bath mat to step on!"

In other ways, though, the shelter was not a bad experience. Melissa shared a room with two other women. One of them quickly became "like a sister." "We were a team," Melissa says. "When I got there with nothing, she gave me everything she could—clothes and the like." To this day, she and her former roommates continue to get together for the occasional meal.

Melissa quickly decided that she was going to put her time in the shelter to good use. She went to the Camden County One Stop Career Center, an organization that connects job seekers with employment, training, and education programs. One Stop helped her sign up for courses to boost her reading and math skills. Eventually, she received a grant to enroll in the Brooks Alternative School in nearby Voorhees to train as a CNA. She completed the 90-hour program in only four weeks, passed her exam to become certified, found a job at a nursing home, got off public assistance, and moved into her own apartment.

Melissa enjoys her work as a CNA, and she recommends the job to others. "If you get your certification, you can find work," she says. "I get texts constantly letting me know about places that are hiring." She points out that CNAs don't even have to have high-school degrees. Melissa is a "people person," and she enjoys interacting with patients, taking special pride in her skill in calming people with mental illness or dementia. She is steadily adding to her skills: right now she is training to operate the EKG machine (a machine that measures the electrical activity of the heart) and to do phlebotomy (drawing blood and preparing it for laboratory testing).

The people Melissa had worked with at One Stop have been so impressed by her rapid progress that they nominated her for an award given out at the annual Garden State Employment and Training Workforce Development conference. There, Melissa told her story to an audience of more than 300 people.

"I don't mind telling people where I came from," she says. "Just like I don't mind telling them where I am going."

Where *is* Melissa going?

She has her sights set on becoming a registered nurse, and eventually a nurse practitioner. Many days she works double shifts in order to save money for her further education.

She knows she has a long way to go. But that doesn't discourage her.

"I came out of that shelter with a plan," she says. "I looked around there, and I saw whole families. I saw pregnant girls, girls with newborn babies. I said, 'That is no way for people to live.' There's no way that's going to be my life.

"If it takes 100 years, I'm going to get my RN degree," says Melissa.

Nobody who knows this determined lady would bet against her. ∎

Suashunn

SUASHUNN Harlan gets straight to the point.

"I am not going to be one more 'nigga that didn't make it out of the hood.'"

Suashunn is about to begin his senior year at the University of California at Berkeley, one of the country's highest-ranking schools. At age 25, Black, and from gritty South Central Los Angeles, Suashunn is not one of the school's more typical students.

"I'm surrounded by people who are unaware of their privilege," he says. "There are a lot of rich white kids who have the attitude, 'We succeeded on our own, so anyone should be able to.' I say, 'No, you didn't succeed *on your own*. Your private tutors and your SAT coaches and your parents' money had *a lot* to do with it.'"

Suashunn didn't have private tutors and SAT coaches. His neighborhood was "typical inner city," rife with drugs and gangs and crime. Suashunn accepted his surroundings as normal. "When you're a kid, you assume everyone lives the way you do," he says. "I never thought, for instance, about not throwing trash in the street. I never thought about having a father. Nobody I knew had a dad. I'd see other ways to live on TV or in the movies, but those were just fantasies. Those stories didn't have anything to do with us."

"Us" was Sua (as his friends call him—pronounced "Swah"), his identical twin Tre'shunn, little brother and sister D'shunn and Calynn, and mom Tracy. As Sua mentioned, his family's story did not resemble the ones he saw on TV. His mom's parents originally lived in the South, where his grandmother died of a heroin overdose when her daughter, Sua's mom, was four. Sua met his father once, when he was about three. "He took Tre and me to the mall," he recalls. "He didn't buy us anything—he just took us."

Despite gang activity all around him, Sua never joined a gang. In his own neighborhood, he didn't get pressured to do so. The reason: "My mom sold drugs," he says, without embarrassment. "She was respected, and so we were pretty much left alone." Outside his neighborhood was a different story. "I'd get banged on," he said, explaining that gang members would ask where he was from in a very intimidating way.

Sua didn't get involved in drugs or crime, either. Instead, he and his twin, Tre, were "not typical Black kids. We were geeks," he says with a chuckle. While many young men turn to gangs for a sense of family, Sua and Tre found their tribe among a group of school friends he lovingly describes as "weirdos." "There was Andrew, who couldn't feel pain. I mean that literally—he had no sense of pain. Rashawn, who loved all this stuff that Black kids don't do, like snowboarding and baseball. Matt was a red-haired super white kid out of a terrible, abusive family. Vance—he was just hella weird. We were nerds. Me, I loved science fiction, horror movies, graphic novels. Any movie with Robert DeNiro in it, I've seen."

Other relatives went a more typical way. Sua remembers his favorite cousin, Emerson. "He was the coolest person ever. He'd come over with his gangbanger friends, and I'd play with their guns. Then somebody got killed, and he's in prison for 15 years."

His mother's involvement with the drug trade was just a fact of life—it was how she supported her family. "She's an awesome mom," Sua emphasizes. "Super loving, kind, generous." Despite the fact that there was crack cocaine in the house, no one in the family used it. "As I grew up, my thoughts were mostly how annoying drug users are," he says. "They'd be knocking at the door at all hours, super fidgety and frantic. I had no interest in trying any hard drugs. I was busy with my video games, great TV and films, and creative writing. Never once did I consider using drugs myself."

The drugs brought more than users to the door. Sua was 13 when the first raid happened. Just before the police burst in, he'd been playing with his BB gun. "I know if I'd still been holding the gun, I'd be dead," he says. Instead, he lay on the floor shouting, "I'm a kid! I'm a kid!" as police trained their weapons on him. His mother went to prison for nine months. During that time, Tre and Sua stayed in the house alone. An uncle brought them groceries.

Even though there were no adults in the house, the twins continued going to school.

At school, Sua passed the subjects he liked— English and history. He didn't understand math at all, but he didn't concern himself with that. "I literally didn't know what the SAT was, or that people took it in order to apply to college," he says. "In fact, I didn't know you had to *apply* to college. I thought people just went, like you go from middle school to high school." Looking back, he is angry at the lack of counseling. "It was very racist, as far as I'm concerned," he says. "The assumption was that poor Black kids weren't college material."

Although he didn't go looking for trouble, trouble occasionally found Suashunn. He had his first encounter with the police when he was about 8.

"I'd gone to the store to get milk," he recalls. "The store was closed. I asked the police officer that did security there what time it opened. He didn't bother to answer; he just shooed me away like I was a dog." Sua responded by raising his middle finger. In response, the grown man came after him, screaming, "You stupid nigger, I'll kill you! I'll shove my nightstick up your ass."

Sua got the message that many young Black men get: the police are the enemy. He saw men in his neighborhood roughed up by police on a regular basis. As a high-school student, he went out with some white friends to shoot their airsoft guns (like fancy BB guns). Before they fired a shot, someone called the police to report that "terrorists" were shooting at cars. "An army of cops, including a helicopter, showed up," Sua remembers. "So we walked up to the cops and— guess what? They talked with my white friends. Me, they put in handcuffs."

The direction of Sua's life began to change when he was in 11th grade. Walking home from school one day, he smelled smoke. A neighbor spotted him and yelled, "Hey, your house burned!" The family had no insurance. His mother borrowed money to repair the damage, and the family had to move in with relatives in another area of Los Angeles.

While he found the area boring—"people went to the mall for fun, and that was about it"—Sua looks back at the fire as a blessing in disguise. He found himself less interested in material belongings, and more thoughtful about the future. Sua focused more on his classes. He still didn't get any encouragement to attend college, but his new teachers showed interest in him, which motivated him to try harder. His grades improved. He took after-school classes and summer courses to make up for classes he'd failed.

High-school graduation came and went. Sua worked at various jobs—in a bookstore, in a movie theater. He continued writing, watching films, playing video games. The family moved back to their original neighborhood and into the repaired house. Sua looked around the area. He was depressed by what he saw.

"Nobody was doing anything of value," he said. "They were having kids, getting pregnant, grinding at dead-end jobs. Just living day by day, with no future." What bothered Sua most was that his peers accepted this lifestyle as normal. "They were content with it," he says. "It was a continuation of the cycle they came from."

He didn't know exactly what he wanted to do, but he knew that he didn't want to be "just a statistic." Sua decided to take a course at Los Angeles Trade Technical College (LATTC). He began with a three-hour math course taught by an instructor with a thick Russian accent.

It didn't go well.

"I took my same crappy high-school attitude into college," he admits. "I didn't understand; I gave up. I failed the course."

But the experience was enough to strike a spark within Suashunn.

His thoughts turned to his mother—an intelligent, hard-working person who had once been offered a full college scholarship. She had passed on that opportunity in favor of the quick money that selling drugs had provided. Then there had been a second police raid on the house, and she'd gotten out of the business. With that loss of income, she couldn't keep up payments on the house. Once again, the family became homeless.

"I had witnessed my mom going from a self-sufficient woman that never needed to ask anyone for anything to a homeless woman begging God for guidance in the middle of the night," Sua says, his voice raw with hurt. "That left a scar on my soul. I decided I was not going to end up like that. I'm going be the one who changes things for my family."

Sua returned to LATTC with a new attitude. Over the next five years, he took classes as he was able. "I figured, 'I'm not married, I don't have kids, I can do this on my own schedule,'" he says. He resolved to make good use of his time in college. He became deeply focused on his studies—editing papers again and again, reading texts and analyzing them critically. For math classes, he found a lifesaving resource—YouTube videos. He'd find an online teacher who explained things clearly and watch and re-watch the videos until he understood the concepts. Eventually, his math skills improved so much that he was able to help other LATTC students with the subject.

By the time Sua earned his associate's degree at LATTC, he had a 4.0 grade point average. Counselors at the college encouraged him to aim high as he applied to four-year schools. The University of California at Berkeley accepts only one in five transfer applicants. Suashunn was one of them. He'll be graduating in 2017 with a degree in social welfare and a minor in creative writing.

While he's happy to be attending a prestigious university, Suashunn is not blind to the way he stands out as a Black man from the 'hood. His voice is bitter as he lists some of the "microaggressions" he experiences on campus.

"Every time I go to the library, I have to show my ID," he says. "White students just walk in, but me? I have to prove that I'm a Berkeley student. White women clutch their purses as I walk by. When I'm with a group of other Black students, I see white people look startled and cross the street to avoid us."

Sua lives in a co-op called Afro House with other Black students. "Being around other intelligent and unique Black individuals helps me keep my sanity," he says. "We share experiences and help each other deal with the pressures." Afro House is about a fifteen-minute walk from campus. There are times when Sua, who enjoys running, would like to run to and from the house, but he doesn't. "Seeing a Black man running scares people, like I'm running away from something or about to do something. So . . . I walk."

Getting a degree from Berkeley isn't going to make Suashunn forget that people of color, especially if they're from poor neighborhoods, are regarded with fear and suspicion by many of their fellow citizens. He's angry about that, and he's not going to let a college degree and a professional career let him forget that anger.

"Black kids are not treated as children in our society," he says. "Whenever my mom and I had to interact with police, they would assume I was her boyfriend, not her child. This was before I was even in my teens. When society teaches you that Black people are violent animals, treating them cruelly becomes second nature."

Suashunn's mom now works as a home health aide. Sua wants more for her, and for all his people.

"My family has nobody successful to look at. Everyone lives on the poverty line," he says. "I'm going to be the one to break that tradition. I will be the reason that our family will have lawyers, doctors, and professors. I'm tired of my people thinking the 'hood is all there is. I am tired of my family working 40 hours a week at minimum wage and thinking that's the best they can do. I have an example to set for my little brother and sister so they can do more than I have and go further than me."

Sua's determination has already born fruit. His twin, Tre, also a rising senior at Berkeley, is doing a summer program at the University of

Michigan. Younger brother D'Shunn, now 23, is studying engineering at LATTC. Little sister Calynn is doing very well in high school—"she's hella smart," says Sua. "She reads a lot more than I do."

As for Sua, he's working as a college adviser at a high school very much like the one he attended. There, he counsels low-income kids on what they need to know to get out of the 'hood and into college. "I'm doing for them what I wish someone had done for me," he says. "It's very, very satisfying work."

He's also on his way to Hong Kong for two months, where a scholarship will allow him to work for a public policy organization and attend university classes. After graduation, he is thinking of applying to law school. He would like to be a human rights attorney, helping people learn how to defend themselves in a system that too often oppresses the poor.

Looking back at his unlikely beginnings, Sua says, "Mom sold drugs. It was what she felt she had to do. But she was also the kindest, most generous person you could ever meet. She raised three sons who aren't in jail and aren't in gangs. She instilled in us a strong will and a resistance to peer pressure. She did a lot of things right."

Like mother, like son. Suashunn Harlan is determined to keep doing things right. ■

Tricia

ALTHOUGH they have been in the United States for only four years, it's hard to tell that the children of Tricia Ofori-Duodu are not native-born Philadelphians. As they tell the story of their arrival from their native Ghana, a country in West Africa, they laugh and joke together, sounding like any group of American kids.

What makes Tricia's children stand out is this: in their four short years in the American school system, each has become an academic star.

Joy, age 18, will be a freshman at Princeton University this fall, where she is thinking of studying English literature. Jude, age 15, is at the top of his class at Central High School and dreams of being an astrophysicist. Joan, 12, is also an excellent student who thinks about going to Stanford University to study fashion design.

The key to the children's success is their mom. A soft-spoken woman with a big smile, Tricia knows that life is filled with challenges and unexpected detours. But she is determined to find the good in every circumstance.

It was one such challenge that inspired her come to the U.S. with her children. "The end of my marriage changed my perspective," she says today. "I passed through a lot and had to take on many responsibilities. Those times were hard, but today I see that if I'd had a very good marriage, I would not be here with these wonderful opportunities for my children."

In order to come to the United States, Tricia had to first enter the "green card lottery" program. After being randomly selected to continue the process, she went through a series of difficult interviews with immigration officials. Finally she got the good news: she and her children would be allowed to come to the United States.

But there was still a problem. The cost of bringing the family to the U.S. would be more than $8,000. Fortunately, Tricia's parents were determined to help their daughter. They sold farmland belonging to the family and took out loans to make the move possible.

The family arrived in the U.S. in September 2010. A family friend, also from Ghana, offered to let Tricia and her children share his home in Philadelphia.

The first weeks were difficult. Although the family was in the United States legally, their friend warned them not to go out in public. He scared them by saying that the police would harass them and make them go back to Ghana. Slowly the family met other Ghanaians who reassured them that their friend was mistaken, and that they could move about freely. In October, Tricia felt confident enough to enroll the children in school.

Eager to support her family and to move into their own apartment, Tricia began working two jobs. She would rise at 3 a.m. to travel to Philadelphia International Airport, where she worked as a restaurant cashier from 4 a.m. until noon. She then took a city bus to her second job at a water ice stand, where she worked from 2 until 8 p.m. She kept up that exhausting schedule for six months, until she had saved enough to move the family to a place of their own.

After cutting back to just one full-time job at the airport, Tricia began to focus on her education. She had attended college in Ghana, but knew she needed to get further training in the American system. She contacted an organization called World Education Services, which helped her convert her Ghanaian diplomas and certificates into forms an American university could accept. She then enrolled at DeVry University, where she is currently working on her bachelor's degree in business. She takes her courses online, two at a time, completing each of them in eight weeks. She is on the dean's list, and she will complete her degree in the fall.

How does she do it all? Tricia admits she doesn't sleep much—no more than five hours a night, except on her days off. Because she also oversees her children's schoolwork, she delays her own studying until they are asleep, and makes use of her 45-minute break at work.

While Tricia was juggling the demands of work and school, her children were experiencing their own challenges as they began school in the U.S. Those issues were more social than academic. All the children were excellent students in Ghana, and all spoke English perfectly. (Because Ghana was once a British colony, English is its "official" language and is spoken in schools. At home, most Ghanaians speak one of nine other African languages.) But when their classmates learned that the children were from Africa, the negative comments began.

For Joy, the first target was her hair. In Ghana, schoolgirls are required to keep their hair very short. Her classmates teased her about looking like a boy. Some fellow students made it clear that they didn't know very much about Africa. During a math class, other students were napping with their heads on their desks. Noticing that Joy was sitting up straight, one student said, "Joy is afraid to go to sleep. She thinks a lion will come out of the jungle and eat her." The other students laughed. Joy did not.

Joy was surprised by her classmates' ignorance about Africa, which is a huge continent made up of more than 50 very different countries. "They would say things to me about 'African food' or 'African clothes' or tell me to 'do that African dance,'" she remembers. "I'd say to them, 'I have lived in *one country* in Africa. They're not all the same!'"

Joy also found it hard to adjust to American food—much of which she still doesn't like! "I've grown to like pizza all right," she says, "but I still eat it with a fork!" She prefers Ghanaian food like *waakye*, a favorite dish of rice and beans topped with a cooked egg.

Jude remembers classmates laughing at his British-accented English and asking ridiculous questions like, "In Africa, did you live in a tree?"

Joan probably had the least difficulty, as she was in elementary school. Younger children were curious about her former home, but not insulting. "They would just ask questions, like 'Where is Ghana? What is it like?'"

But all of Tricia's children have inherited their mother's determination. They would not let other people's nonsense distract them from their goal: to make the most of the opportunities before them. Within months, all three of the kids were making excellent grades and proving to be natural leaders.

The teasing soon slowed down. "Maybe my classmates didn't respect Africa," says Jude, "but they respected straight A's. They started coming to me for help with their homework."

Through her children's school counselors, Tricia learned about a program that was ideally suited for her children. Philadelphia Futures is a program that helps low-income kids with high potential prepare for success in college. It matches students with mentors, takes them on trips to visit colleges, provides academic support, and helps students apply for scholarships. Joy and Jude are both deeply involved with Philly Futures, and Joan is looking forward to joining the program when she reaches high school. Joy comments that joining the program helped her feel more at home in the United States. "I met other students who had goals similar to mine, and they became my friends." In her senior year in high school, Joy won the Philadelphia Futures Outstanding Achievement award—the organization's highest honor for a high-school student.

The children are making the most of every opportunity in their adopted country. In doing so, they are clearly following the example of their extraordinary mother. Many people who are juggling college classes and parenthood would think of working as a cashier at an airport store simply as a means to a paycheck. But Tricia's determination to find good in all things gives her a different perspective. She thinks of her job as a kind of mission.

"Travel can be very stressful—I know this!" she says with a laugh. "People's flights are delayed, or they're worried about something, and they can be very irritated or frustrated. So when they come into the store, I try to give them a good smile, to help them find what they need quickly. I do what I can to add some beauty to their day."

Sometimes, Tricia admits, it is she who is frustrated and stressed. She works long hours; she worries about her children meeting friends who are "not on the right track"; she is treated rudely at times by customers who notice her accent and will not try to communicate with her. "There are people who say 'I can't understand you' and walk away. That's very painful.

"But if I'm sad, what will my children do?"

Tricia looks forward to the day when she can give back to Philadelphia Futures, the organization that has helped support her children on their journey to success. Someday she hopes to Sponsor a Scholar—be a person whose donation allows a specific student to prepare effectively for college.

Given Tricia's record of determination, it's a good bet she will reach that goal. ■

Richard

"THEY *tried to make me go to rehab I said 'no, no, no.'"*
"Rehab," Amy Winehouse

Like singer Amy Winehouse, Richard Grant didn't want to go to rehab. But given a choice between rehab and six years in prison, he went. Looking back, he sees his time in rehab as the most valuable experience of his life.

Richard grew up in Camden, New Jersey. He was a bright kid with plenty of potential and a supportive family, but he couldn't seem to get his life together. "I just wanted to play basketball and video games," he remembers. By the time he was in seventh grade, he had pretty well stopped attending school. "I was being bullied," Richard says. "My mom complained, but the school seemed to consider me the problem."

He pauses for a moment and then adds, "Actually, I *was* a problem. I did get teased. But I couldn't control my temper. Looking back, I can understand why they wanted me out."

Notice the way that Richard interrupted himself, went back, and took partial blame for the school situation. His ability to do that—to review his life and admit that he played a role in creating his problems—helps explain how Richard, now 37, has been able to turn his life around.

After quitting school, Richard bounced around for a few years. He tried once to enroll in a technical school, but his records were missing, and he gave up. He enrolled in the Youth Corps for work training and to earn his GED (General Education Development degree—the equivalent of a high-school diploma), but failed that test and, again, gave up. Meanwhile, he began fathering children—by 2002, there were four. He worked dead-end jobs—fast food, loading docks, warehouses—that paid minimum wage. To help support his children, and to pay for his own marijuana habit, he started selling drugs.

"My get-rich-quick scheme," he says, with a wry smile. "It got me rich with trouble."

Before long, Richard was arrested. When he was convicted of selling drugs, he was given two options: a six-year prison sentence (with possibility of parole after ten months), or six months of rehab and then "drug court."

As Richard learned, drug court is a program aimed at helping people convicted of non-violent drug-related crimes break the cycle of addiction and crime. Rather than just punishing the offender, drug court brings together law enforcement, medical supervisors, and social services agencies to work with the individual. The goal is that the person will come away from drug court with the skills and the desire to "go straight."

While it may sound like an easy alternative to prison, drug court is tough.

For Richard, it began with six months of in-patient rehab. After that came five years of closely supervised parole, with frequent court appearances, attendance at programs, and frequent urine tests to check for drug use. If Richard had violated his parole at any point during those five years—for example, if he had had a "dirty" test—he would have been required to serve his original prison sentence.

Richard didn't slip up. But that doesn't mean he was happy about the program, especially when he first began rehab.

"I bitched and moaned for the first three months," he admits. "But then I began to . . . get it. I listened to other people's stories, and I heard my own words and my own excuses coming back at me. Gradually, I learned to own up to my own actions. I looked back at my life, saw my 'misfortunes,' and saw that I'd set them all up to happen."

As a result, he learned a valuable skill.

"I developed a mental tape, a tape that I play in my head when I'm facing a decision," he says. "I say, OK, if I do A, what is going to happen? And I look ahead to B and C and so on. I don't just live in the present, saying 'Whatever.' I look into the future and make my decisions accordingly. I make a plan to get where I want to go."

By the time Richard finished rehab, he looked at it as "the best thing I've ever done."

Not only did rehab and drug court convince Richard that he wanted to stay out of trouble—it made him start thinking about a career. He was deeply interested in drug and alcohol treatment, and disgusted with the traditional "lock 'em up" way of dealing with addicts who commit crimes.

"The judicial system doesn't have any answers for addiction," he says. "It just puts people away for the moment, instead of focusing on treatment. And the addiction just lies there, dormant, if it isn't treated. People don't get better in prison. If anything, they get worse."

He'd continued to work at low-level jobs, but at least Richard had stepped up from the bottom rung. He worked for two years at a Checkers restaurant, becoming a manager, but when that restaurant was taken over by its parent corporation, he had to reapply for the job he already had. He was turned down because of his drug conviction. Instead, he was offered a job as a crew member for seven dollars an hour.

Richard felt angry and disappointed. But losing his manager's job made him realize two things. He really wanted a career, not just a job. And to prepare for a career, he had to go back to school.

At that point, Richard's newfound determination pushed him into action. He was already familiar with Carol Dann, the director of the Camden County Adult Basic Skills (CCABS) program. Because he was receiving state assistance, he was required to participate in CWEP—the Community Worker Employment Program. His work assignment was in Carol's office, where he did tasks such as filing and making copies. Carol had put in a good word for

Richard at a local supermarket, where he began working in the deli. Now, he enrolled in CCABS as a student and earned his GED in the summer of 2014. With his high-school degree in hand, he immediately enrolled at Camden County Community College. He's well on his way to earning an associate's degree—and he's on the dean's list. His plan is to earn a certificate in drug and alcohol counseling. After that, he hopes to continue in college, perhaps to become a licensed social worker.

In the meantime, Richard is done with dead-end jobs. Now that he's going to college at night, he works days as a technician at a plant that develops resins used in such applications as dialysis machines, water softening, and pollution control. "It's actually fun!" Richard says. "A lot more interesting that working on a loading dock."

Richard earned his GED just before his oldest child, now 18, graduated from high school. "I couldn't let him get out of high school before I did!" Richard says. He wants his children to learn from his experience and understand the value of education. "I tell them, education and experience are things that can't be taken from you. Someone can always take your job. But if you have training and skills, you can take those to another position, rather than feeling like you've lost everything. You'll still be in control of your life." ■

Crystal

CRYSTAL Delmonico would be the first to tell you that, for much of her 37 years, she was a mess.

By the time she was in middle school, she was drinking regularly. She was so disruptive she was often kicked out of the classroom. In eighth grade, she dropped LSD at school and "went insane." After turning 13, she rarely lived at home. Instead, she bounced between rehab facilities, psychiatric hospitals, and group homes. After high school, there were periods of homelessness, days spent in crack houses, and thoughts of suicide.

In her words, "I created chaos wherever I went."

But today, Crystal is a graduate of Community College of Philadelphia. More surprisingly, in the fall, she will transfer to one of the most selective colleges in the country: the University of Pennsylvania. She has been sober for almost five years. She lives in South Philadelphia, in a subsidized apartment for people with disabilities, with her cat, Sheena. Proudly gay, she has a circle of supportive friends and colleagues, all cheering her on as she moves towards her goal of helping kids who are as lost as she once was.

Looking back at her own troubled past, Crystal sees that her behavior made sense, in a crazy sort of way.

"As I kid, I was told I had lied about bad things that had happened to me," she says. "That really messed me up. When you learn that you can't trust your own memories, and that you are not safe—that's hard to cope with. My response was to get angry and get high."

Crystal was about 8 when she was sexually abused by a trusted family member. At that age, she did not really understand what had happened. It wasn't until she was 12 that she mentioned the situation to an adult neighbor. The woman was clearly shocked. She told Crystal, "Grownups aren't supposed to do that." Crystal was contacted by child welfare authorities. She panicked, thinking that she'd done something wrong. She was afraid she would be blamed for getting the adult into trouble. So she denied the story, telling the authorities that nothing had happened after all. But to her family, she told the truth—that she had really been molested.

Her family said she was lying. Years later, certain relatives admitted that they had believed her, but that they thought "keeping peace in the family" was more important than supporting her.

Even now, Crystal looks bewildered as she says, "Why would a little kid make that up?"

As Crystal grew older, she tried to put the incident out of her mind. But the pressure of pretending things were OK when she felt so hurt and betrayed kept eating at her. She found that drinking and using drugs helped block the bad thoughts, at least for a while. She became a troublemaker at school, one who would show up drunk and get into fights. A learning disability made it difficult for her to do well in some classes, especially math. Embarrassed when she couldn't do the work, she would deliberately get herself thrown out of class. "I knew exactly what I had to do to get kicked out," she says today, a guilty grin on her face. "I'd mouth off, act out, *just* enough."

Although teachers found her frustrating, Crystal also was aware of something that continued to be true throughout her troubled years. Many teachers liked her and wanted to be supportive. "I had one math teacher, a Vietnam vet, who had been injured and had a metal plate in his jaw," Crystal remembers. "The plate made it painful for him to laugh. He told me later that even though it hurt, I could always make him laugh. He really tried to help me, but I wouldn't let him. School was just not a priority."

Crystal was in seventh grade when her parents sent her to rehab for alcohol abuse. She spent thirty days in a residential facility, and then attended outpatient sessions. That was the first of many trips to rehab over the next twenty years. After each program, she would stay sober briefly, then relapse.

"Why did I drink?" she asked. "I drank so the chatter in my head would shut up. I felt hopeless and lost and scared. Drinking took me out of that, for a little while."

At the beginning of eighth grade, a concerned teacher had a talk with Crystal. He told her that, as a child, he had been sexually abused. As he saw Crystal doing crazy, self-destructive things, he wondered if the same thing had happened to her. She told him it had. With his encouragement, she went to the school guidance counselor and told her story. The police got involved. They interviewed Crystal and others.

But at the end of their investigation, the authorities said that Crystal had made the story up.

For Crystal, this was a kick in the gut. She had done the right thing. She had told the truth. But once again, she hadn't been believed.

Her behavior went downhill. The LSD incident at school ended up with her locked in a psychiatric hospital for several months. She lived for two years at the Hoffman Homes for Youth near Gettysburg, Pennsylvania. There she met the director's wife, another adult who believed in her and pushed her to believe in herself. Crystal keeps a scrapbook of her time at the Homes. It includes this poem that she wrote for the woman:

I looked for the worst in me,
and you looked for the best . . .

I saw no hope in the future,
and you showed there was . . .

I felt the badness inside,
and you brought out the goodness . . .

When I went through the troubled times
you gave me compassion . . .

You were there to laugh with,
but you also helped show me
seriousness in things too . . .

You've made a difference in my life.
Not seen by the eye but felt by the heart.

And I want to thank you.
'Cause I owe it all to you . . .

There were times Crystal's natural ability came to the surface. She returned home for her senior year in high school and did pretty well, even taking some honors classes. "There was actual money bet among the teachers about whether I'd graduate," she remembers. "When I walked across the stage and got my diploma, a lot of teachers stood up and clapped. I guess they're the ones who won the bet!"

The day after graduation, Crystal moved out of her parents' home. Since no one was keeping an eye on her, her drinking and drug use increased. Sometimes she lived in Philadelphia with a friend, also an addict. She worked off and on at a pizza restaurant. She went in and out of rehab programs. At times she lived out of her old station wagon. Certain moments made her feel sick with shame. One occurred when she woke up in her car to hear a family playing ball nearby. As she emerged from the back seat, dragging her sleeping bag, the father of the family grabbed the children and hurried them away from her. "I was so humiliated to realize how I looked to them," she remembers. During another period, her addict roommate had kicked her out of his apartment. Crystal and another friend wandered the streets together, sleeping in Washington Park or Rittenhouse Square. One night it rained heavily. Crystal still had a key to her former friend's apartment. Knowing his work schedule, she and her friend let themselves into his building when he was away and hid in the basement, trying to get some sleep on the filthy dirt floor.

"It was a . . . moment," Crystal says today, struggling to find the right word. "I thought, 'I can't do this anymore.'" Through all the confusion and depression and the fog of substance abuse, something new began to grow: a sense of determination. Somehow, Crystal knew, she had to get out of this mess.

She began to look for help—real help, not the revolving door of rehab programs she'd been through so many times. Crystal knew that her drinking and drug use were serious problems, but that they were not the only issues that were damaging her life. She had been diagnosed with Attention Deficit Hyperactivity Disorder (ADHD) and post-traumatic stress disorder (PTSD).

It is PTSD that Crystal believes was running her life. It is a condition that can develop after a person has experienced a very upsetting situation, such as being a crime victim or being in combat. Sexual abuse victims are also at risk. People with PTSD can experience extremely anxiety, flashbacks, nightmares, aggression, and a sense of unreality, as if they are living in a dream. Those symptoms describe how Crystal felt much of the time. She believes that the traumatic experience of being abused, and then being told that her experience wasn't real, led to her developing PTSD.

Crystal's search for healing was not a straight or an easy path. She went first to the Hall-Mercer Community Behavioral Health Center of Pennsylvania Hospital and worked with a caseworker there. She moved on to Project HOME, a shelter for formerly homeless people. After a year and a half in the shelter, she received residential care from "Women of Hope," another organization that helps homeless women with mental health problems. At each step along the way, she learned more about how to cope with PTSD and the rages, depression, and anxiety that came with it.

There were setbacks. For stretches during this period, she stayed sober. Several times she "fell off the wagon." But she didn't give up. "I'd had a taste of a healthy, sober life," she says. "I knew that being permanently sober was the only way I could survive."

At moments, Crystal wasn't sure she wanted to survive. During one very low period, she visited a church she had once been involved with. She knew some people there who seemed kind and caring. On the train to the church, she prayed. "I said, 'I need help. I need hope. I need people in my life,'" she recalls. "But the church people basically said, 'Don't be gay anymore. Walk away from your gay friends. If you stop being gay, we can accept you and help you.'"

Crystal felt heartbroken. She had always believed in God, and she did not believe that he loved her any less for being gay. That day, waiting for the train to take her back to Philadelphia, she thought about stepping onto the tracks and ending her life.

At that very moment, her phone rang. It was a friend she hadn't spoken to for a long time. "She was someone who I could see had peace in her life," Crystal remembers. "I wanted that." As they talked, the friend told Crystal about what had helped her: learning to meditate.

Meditation wasn't an entirely new idea to Crystal. She had tried to meditate, on her own, not long before. But sitting quietly, alone with her thoughts, was torture. "I ended up lying in a fetal position on the floor, sobbing," she said. "The pain was too much."

But after this conversation, Crystal decided

to give meditation another try—not alone, but with a group that could help her learn the technique and deal with the feelings that came up. She began meeting with a group to study Vipassana, an ancient Indian technique that centers on "mindfulness." Mindfulness is a term used to describe focusing one's awareness on the present moment, calmly accepting one's feelings, without judging them as good or bad.

Crystal had spent much of her life agonizing over her past, trying to escape her "bad" thoughts, and worrying about the future. For her, meditation was, literally, a lifesaver. As she sat in silence, focusing on her breath, noticing when her body tensed, accepting her thoughts and then returning to the present moment, she experienced a sense of peace and comfort. Eager to learn more about meditation, she enrolled in an eight-week Mindfulness-Based Stress Reduction course at Jefferson University Hospital. Later, she attended a ten-day silent retreat in Massachusetts. Of the retreat, she says, "It was the best thing I've ever done for myself. It's amazing how much you can learn by not speaking, just by being.

"Meditation let me see that the bad things I tell myself, the self-hatred, those are all meaningless. All that matters is now, this minute. I don't need to revert to acting out, getting angry, getting high."

Crystal began to feel increasingly hopeful about the future. That hope hung on even through another serious crisis: She was diagnosed with cardiomyopathy, a disease of the heart muscle. She had open-heart surgery and continues to deal with congestive heart failure (a condition where the heart doesn't pump blood as well as it should). But instead of sliding back into depression, she felt her determination to do something positive with her life grow stronger. She asked herself, "Why not go back to school?"

"Going through the Jefferson mindfulness program had made me realize, 'This is what I want to do with my life,'" she says. "I want to teach lost, angry kids to use mindfulness. I want to show them that meditation isn't some kind of New Agey, woo-woo thing. There's been so much research on its benefits—how it reduces stress and even physical pain. But to teach it on the level that I want to, I need a graduate degree."

She didn't have any money. But instead of giving up her idea, she did research into financial aid at the Community College of Philadelphia. She was happy to learn she was eligible for grants to pay for her classes. She enrolled at CCP, where she studied liberal arts. Physically, she sometimes struggled. Her heart disease can leave her breathless, unable to ride her bike to class or climb stairs. But she made every effort to get to class. Despite her challenges, she stayed mentally healthy and positive, and she blossomed as a student. She was never ashamed to ask for help, gladly using the college's tutoring center and enlisting a friend to coach her in math. By utilizing all the help available to her, she graduated from CCP with a 3.8 grade point average.

Now, sober and confident, with her associate's degree in hand, Crystal is headed to the University of Pennsylvania. There, finances will be more of a challenge. Costs at Penn amount to about $14,000 a semester. She's received grants and scholarships that will cover about $10,000 of that, leaving her owing $4,000 per semester. She continues to apply for scholarships, hoping to reduce that amount, but she knows she'll have to end up borrowing some of it. "Hey, if I end up borrowing $8,000 a year to attend an Ivy League university, I can live with that," she says.

At Penn, she will study Positive Psychology—a form of psychology that emphasizes mindfulness and "the science of happiness." Eventually she hopes to get a master's degree in social work. From there, she says, "I want to help kids who feel as hopeless as I did to experience the freedom I have today. I want them to realize they can have joy in their lives." ■

Juan

MY name is Juan Angel. I am thirty years old, and I was born in Mexico.

As a child, I was alone for most of the time. It did not seem that I had a bright future. My father was an alcoholic, and he left my family and me when I was three years old. My mother had to struggle to survive by working from place to place in Mexico. Her effort to support me was not enough because of low salaries, so she left to work in the United States.

I lived with some of my relatives in a little village in Mexico and worked from dawn to sunset and ate sometimes once a day. I felt I would die of starvation and hard work. My relatives spent the money that my mother sent me. They claimed that I was just a child and didn't need it. As a child, I was not able to resist. After five years of being mistreated by my relatives, I left them. I went to live with my grandmother, who lived in another village.

When I moved into my grandmother's house, I started a new life. By then, I was eight years old. I felt proud of myself for the first time because I had made my first big decision in life. I was only a little boy, but I think I knew I could have a better life if I was determined.

My grandmother had some pigs, so I had to feed them. One day I was feeding them close to a water stream when I saw two boys passing by. They carried some books with them. I saw them every day walking down a grassy road while I fed those pigs. My curiosity grew, and one day I stopped them on their way back home. I asked them what they were doing, and they told me that they were attending school. I wanted to know if they knew how to read, and they started reading and writing to show me. I simply couldn't believe it. When they left, I scratched my head and nodded for a moment, looking toward the sky. I said, "Going to school! That's the next step I have to work on." After I finished feeding those pigs, I went home. While I was walking home, I thought about how I would get my grandmother to allow me to go to school. I knew it was going to be hard to do. There were around twenty boys in the village, and only the two I met were going to school. But if they could do it, why couldn't I?

I knew what I wanted to do. But my grandmother wanted me to stay with the pigs. So for two years I stayed with her before taking my next step. But I did not forget my resolve. I then left my grandmother and found a place to sleep in the town where the school was. The two boys I knew took me to the school, and I told my story to the principal. His name was Juan, also. I told him I was determined to get an education. He told me that my age (ten years old) made me too old to come to the school. But then he spoke with his teachers, and they all agreed to let me enter. They knew my desire to learn was great.

A week later my grandmother found me. I cried while I explained to her why I had left home. She understood. She hugged me very hard, and then she went to talk to the principal and gave her approval. I returned to live with her and walked the two miles back and forth to school every day. I had to feed the pigs early in the morning before I went to school and after I came home from school. I also chopped wood for cooking and did other chores as well. I was a responsible man in charge of a household. I was proud that I had stuck to my resolution to go to school. My grandmother and I lived happily for six years while I was in primary school.

After I finished my first six years in school, I had to make another tough decision. The secondary school I wished to attend was in a town about three hours away by bus. I hated to leave my grandmother, but I wanted to stay in school. I visited her weekends when I had enough money to do so. By the start of my second year in the school, I began to worry about her health and the bad chest pains she felt in her heart.

One day a friend of mine came looking for me at the school. He told me that my grandmother was very sick. I at once returned to see her. She was lying down with a blanket on the floor. When she saw me, she hugged me very hard. Then she began to ask how my school was. I could hardly answer her because tears ran down my cheeks as never before. She asked me not to cry, but I couldn't stop. She told me to continue in school, and I promised her I would. A few minutes later, she died in my arms. I felt that everything was torn apart inside me. I thought that I could never overcome the painful experience of losing my grandmother. But I never regretted my decision to stay in school.

My mother, who was here in the United States, got there in time for the funeral. She asked me to go back with her, but I refused her offer. So she returned to the United States, and I stayed in Mexico for another four years of school. She continued asking me to join her. Finally, I moved to the United States. I took English classes at night and worked days. My English teacher told me about a Hispanic program where I could get my GED diploma. I became determined to achieve this new goal. There was no stopping me: I finished the program and earned my GED. Soon after, I started working on a farm, growing alfalfa. I worked three years, and then I quit to find a more flexible job so I could attend college.

Now I'm working in a feed department on a swing shift, and I'm a student at Blue Mountain Community College in the mornings. I have dealt with many obstacles in my life since childhood, and I have overcome them. It has not been easy, but I believe in success through education. Even though I know the struggle is not over yet, I will keep a hopeful smile toward the future. I know that as long as I stay strong, no one can stop me.

AN UPDATE

It's been 20 years since the editors at Townsend Press talked with Juan Angel. They contacted him recently at his home in Stanfield, Oregon, to see where those two decades had taken him.

No longer a farm worker, Juan built and opened his own auto repair shop in 2000. The experience of constructing a commercial building interested him, and he began to invest in real estate—buying properties, fixing them up, and reselling them. Eventually he became a licensed real-estate broker, working to help local Hispanic people buy and sell their homes. "Between the auto business and real estate, I'm not rich, but I'm surviving!" he says. His wife, Hilda, manages the kitchen at a local motel. Youngest son Juan Jr. is studying mechanical engineering at Walla Walla University; older son Danny is a supervisor at a supermarket. Daughter Vianey, who earned a master's degree in social work and works at a hospital in Seattle, is married. "She's just told us she's going to make me a grandpa!" Juan reports happily.

The 20 years have not been without their difficult times. Struggles with money and family responsibilities made it impossible for Juan to stay in college. At one point, he fell into alcoholism, but proudly reports that he's had ten years of sobriety.

Juan and Hilda are planning a trip to Mexico, where Hilda's mother still lives. In all these years, this will be only his second return to his home country. The first occurred after he'd been in the United States for 26 years. "There were only a few old men in our village who still remembered me," he says. This trip, however, will be longer, and he plans to spend time with some of his old schoolmates. "We've got our plane tickets, so we're ready!"

The little village boy who resolved to get an education has come a long way. ∎

Amanda

"FIRE! Wake up!" screamed Amanda, shaking her little sister, Jessica.

Someone had set a fire in the trashcan in the girls' bedroom. Running into the hallway, Amanda yelled, "Mommy, our room is on fire." Her mother rushed into the bedroom, grabbed the bedspread, and smothered the fire. As she opened a window, she called to her three sons.

Gathering her five children around her, she stared at her oldest son, John, who was looking at the floor.

Amanda whimpered, "He said he would set the house on fire, and he did."

"John, go to my room and sit on the bed. The rest of you, come listen to me. I'll take care of John. You're safe, thanks be to Jesus. Don't worry, now. We're in God's hands, and it won't happen again." Then, turning to nine-year-old Amanda, she asked, "Why didn't you tell me he said he would burn the house down?"

"I thought he was kidding," Amanda answered.

Their mother sighed. "Luke and Matthew, go back to your room," she said. "Amanda and Jessica, sit on my lap for a second. You know, John is a little sick and sometimes does things he shouldn't. I'll talk to some people tomorrow to see what we can do for him, but lie down now, and I'll sing you a song and rub your backs." The girls drifted off to sleep as their mother sang "Don't Let Nobody Turn Me Around," nice and slow, almost a murmur.

Amanda's mother taught her something that night. It was this: No matter how terrible or frightening the world can be, take action to make things better. Get up, put out the fire, and open the window. Do your best to set things right, and if you can do it with heartfelt love, all the better.

Her mother had been taking action for as long as Amanda could remember. Amanda's father had abandoned them shortly after Jessica was born, leaving her mother to hold the family together on welfare checks and food stamps. Her mother never complained, even though her son Matthew was autistic and her oldest, John, displayed scary, violent tendencies. Amanda learned iron-willed determination from her mother and how to respond when life begins to steal your breath away. You get up off the floor and act.

As a middle child, Amanda had always competed with her siblings for her mother's attention. She was first to snuggle next to her mother when she called the children together to read them a bedtime story or tell them a Bible story. When Amanda memorized the words from the few books in the house, her mother was so proud that Amanda learned most of the alphabet by the time she was five. When she came home from kindergarten with smiley-face stickers on her work, her mother said playfully, "Oh, Manda Panda, you are so Miss Smarty Pants!" and gave her a hug. School became the way to earn attention and praise from her mother—and her teachers too. In a large family with an absentee father, it was Amanda's way of taking action, with the reward being her mother's praise. Years later, the work ethic she developed during these early years helped her face severe trials—always with determination.

Amanda's mother made sure the children were safe in their home and, as much as possible, in their neighborhood. Growing up in North Philadelphia wasn't easy. The children could play only on their block and were not allowed to go outside after dark. At the occasional echo of a gunshot, the children dove onto the floor, away from the windows, just as their mother had taught them. They did not have bicycles because, besides the cost, there was no place to ride them safely nor even room to store them in their home.

On the other hand, Amanda's mother encouraged the children to participate in safe, fun activities. For her part, Amanda joined a few after-school, weekend, and summer programs. One of her favorites was the Mural Arts program for children, which allowed her, with supervision, to fill in a stenciled small tree on the side of a building.

One explanation, then, for the grit Amanda would later show in getting her college degree was the determination her mother displayed through her loving, never-give-up attitude.

Religion was another source of strength and determination, helping Amanda to persist when she reached what for others would be a breaking point. Her mother quoted the Bible often, told the children Bible stories, and sang them spirituals. She taught them to rely on God for strength when disasters befell them and made sure they attended Bible study and church every Sunday. They would march down the center aisle, their faces scrubbed and shining, their clothes clean and shoes polished. Her mother told them, "Remember Jesus, and He'll remember you."

Amanda absorbed her mother's lessons, praying every morning and evening. Her belief that God was watching over her made her strong. Just as Amanda had memorized words from her storybooks, she memorized passages from the Bible. Her favorite quotation from Scripture was Philippians 4:13: "I can do all things through Christ who strengtheneth me." Amanda found herself reciting this verse whenever she began to doubt herself. Her strong religious beliefs helped give her the determination and perseverance she would need later when she faced adversity.

Two years after the fire, when Amanda was only 11, her strength and will were put to the hardest test. Her mother was lying on the couch. She called to Amanda, her voice strange and small.

"Call 911," her mother whispered. "I can't breathe."

That night Amanda's life changed. After calling the police, she and her siblings waited anxiously for the ambulance, fanning their mother with a newspaper to help her breathe. Her mother was rushed to the hospital. A few hours later, she was dead.

At the funeral service, with the smell of dead roses in the air, Amanda was numb, not believing her mother was gone, forever. Her brother Luke stood over the coffin with his fists clenched and then, when he was led back to the pew, rocked back and forth for the entire service. Jessica wept quietly. Although Amanda was usually an enthusiastic singer, this day she could not bring herself to join in as the choir sang "I'll Fly Away." She could only ask herself, "Why, Jesus? Why did you take my mommy?" She remembered her mother reading the Bible to them and talking about the bitter drink of suffering that Jesus spoke of. She thought, "Now I know what bitter means." Hoping for strength, she recited her quotation from Philippians 4:13, but she felt drained and uncertain whether she could go on.

For all of her 11 years, despite what she later came to recognize as extreme poverty, Amanda had felt loved and secure in her mother's arms. Like most of the children on her block, she didn't realize she was poor, because everyone in the neighborhood was poor as well. She wasn't bothered by the cramped rooms or by having to share a bedroom with her sister. She didn't care about the thrift-store clothing, the day-old bread, or the mismatched dinner plates, glasses, and silverware. The only thing that really bothered her was being allowed only one glazed donut after church on Sundays, but she knew her mother loved her and would have given her more if she was able. But now her mother was gone.

As Amanda walked out of the church on the day of the funeral, she questioned what her mother had said about God's plan. How could He have let this happen? But as they traveled to the cemetery, she took comfort in remembering that her mother was in heaven and watching over her. This time, when she said, "I can do all things through Christ who strengtheneth me," she believed it. She thought about the night of the fire and how her mother had saved her. Amanda would be like her mother, staying strong for her family. She bit her lip, out of sorrow, but also out of determination to help her family get through this trial.

Amanda knew things would change—and they did. She and her sister Jessica were taken to one emergency foster home, while her brothers went to another. This was the first of four different foster homes for Amanda and her sister. Having assumed the role of mother for Jessica, Amanda was determined to be strong, even as she yearned to have her brothers with them under one roof. She stayed in school, earning good grades, because she knew that was what her mother and God would want her to do.

After a few years, Amanda was finally reunited with her brothers when an aunt agreed to take all four children into her house. (Brother John had been sent to a residential program for troubled children.) "Now," thought Amanda, "we can be a family again."

It soon became apparent to Amanda, however, that living with her aunt would not be what she had hoped. The aunt was chilly and unloving, and Amanda suspected she was more interested in the fee she received from the Department of Human Services than in the children. When they moved into their new home, the aunt announced some odd house rules. "We keep the cabinet doors and the refrigerator locked, so eat when we have meals," she explained. "You can use our house phone only for emergencies. Don't touch the radio or the TV—I select the music. You can attend only schools in this neighborhood. The doors will be locked at 7 each night. After that, you will have to wait to get into the house until your cousin drives me to work at 9 or when he returns after 11."

Amanda asked, "Can't we have a key to let ourselves in and out?"

"No, you don't need a key."

A few years later, Amanda returned home from an evening program at her high school one December evening with a cold drizzle falling, only to find she was locked out. Amanda had to sit on the stoop for two hours. She tightened her jacket, avoiding eye contact with people walking by, and hoped no one would bother her until her cousin returned with the key at 11:00.

Lying in bed that first night in her aunt's house, Amanda heard her sister crying next to her. "It's okay, Jessica. God's watching over us," Amanda said. She hugged her sister and added, "Just think of good things." Amanda comforted herself by remembering the Sunday dinners her mother had prepared for them; the times her mother, holding her hand, walked with her to the neighborhood store for bread and milk; or her mother stroking her hair as she praised Amanda for her school work. She recalled that shortly before her mother died, as she was reviewing Amanda's report card, she told Amanda to keep up her grades so that she could go to college. When Amanda began to reply, "If I go to college . . . ," her mother jumped in, "No, not '*if* you go to college.' It's *when* you go to college. It would be a sin to waste your brains." In bed that first night in her aunt's house, Amanda thought, "Yes,

Mommy, I will go to college. Give me strength." She would set a good example for her brothers and sister, she said to herself as she nodded off to sleep.

Despite her unhappiness at her aunt's house, Amanda was resolved to be the student her mother would have wanted her to be. She studied, listened to her teachers, and earned very good grades. As she completed eighth grade, it was time for her to choose a high school. Although she had hoped to attend Central High School, one of the top schools in Philadelphia, her aunt insisted she choose either a large public high school three blocks from her house or a smaller magnet high school two blocks away. Amanda chose the magnet school because of its size, reputation, and emphasis on the humanities.

Once there, Amanda excelled, continuing the habits she had developed in elementary school. She developed a circle of friends and found some supportive teachers who helped her believe she could make something of herself. She focused on communications, eventually becoming the morning broadcaster on the PA system and a film archivist for school events. She never missed a day of school—perfect attendance. She won awards and had several internships with programs such as Philadelphia Work Ready and Drexel University's Philadelphia Unemployment Project. Her high school recognized her efforts by giving her tickets to see the Jonas Brothers.

Still, she could hardly bear living with her aunt. Things got worse when the aunt kicked Jessica out of the house for talking back to her, sending Jessica to another foster home. It broke Amanda's heart. She visited Jessica on weekends, and was outraged when Jessica confided that the son of her foster parent, Mrs. Walker, was touching her inappropriately.

"Did you tell Mrs. Walker?" Amanda asked.

Jessica answered, "I did, but nothing happened."

Amanda tried to be tactful when she spoke to the foster mom, but Mrs. Walker became defensive. The conversation turned into a shouting match, with Amanda calling the son a child molester and the mother slapping Amanda. When the police arrived, Amanda was told to leave.

Jessica was moved to another foster home. Amanda was upset because Jessica's accusation was never investigated. She told her sister, "Not only are we parentless foster children, but we're also voiceless." That was a defining moment in Amanda's life. Getting into college and graduating was not just a personal goal; it became her mission. All the terrible events in her life wouldn't stop her. She was determined to show her siblings how to fight back in a world of injustice.

So, along with her mother's example and her faith in God, some of Amanda's determination arose from encounters with a system that ignored the poor and defenseless.

At the beginning of Amanda's senior year of high school, her counselor met with her to discuss her plans. "Amanda, what college do you want to attend?" Amanda remembered her mother saying, "*When* you go to college," but she faltered with her answer, knowing there was no way she could pay for a four-year college.

"It's kinda expensive," she answered.

The counselor said, "Yes, but there are scholarships for hard-working students like you. You'll have to borrow some, it's true, but you can definitely attend college."

A few weeks later, a representative of La Salle University visited Amanda's high school to talk about scholarship and academic programs for highly motivated students. Amanda hadn't gotten the highest SAT scores—not terrible, but not terrific either. But the La Salle representative described a program that gave scholarships to excellent students who had a history of hard work, good grades, and volunteer work or school activities, but not high SAT's. Excited by this news, Amanda applied for the program. After visiting the La Salle campus, taking some tests in math and reading, and interviewing, she was accepted. She received a grant package of over $30,000 a year and would have to borrow only a few thousand dollars each year to cover tuition.

Amanda was eager to move out of her aunt's house. As a freshman at La Salle, she got a part-time job at a discount store. Later she added a weekend job at a Lowe's home-improvement store. Once she felt confident she could handle her half of the rent, she found a roommate to share an apartment near the college campus.

Unfortunately Amanda's roommate, Trisha, did not share Amanda's sense of responsibility. Perhaps it was because Trisha was used to receiving support from her parents, while Amanda knew the only help she could expect was what she could give herself. For a few months the two girls shared costs, but then at the Christmas break, Trisha disappeared. Amanda was now responsible for the entire monthly rent. Panicked by the possibility of being homeless, Amanda spoke to one of her college counselors and was awarded a one-time grant of $500 to help pay the rent for January and February. She added more hours at Lowe's, making her almost a full-time employee but earning just minimum wage. It was a stressful time, with Amanda often skipping meals and not buying needed medicine in order to pay her rent and buy textbooks. She had little time for a social life either, and could not enjoy the bonding with friends that is one of the pleasures of attending college.

Despite the stress, the long hours of work at Lowe's, and the demands of college, Amanda persevered, relying on her faith in God. She continued to attend church in order to sing gospel music and praise dance. In quiet times she whispered, "Thank you Mommy, and thank you Jesus."

After graduation, Amanda gave her notice at Lowe's and accepted a full-time position at a large insurance company in center city Philadelphia. She is taking insurance classes paid for by her company, has friends at her firm, and enjoys the work. In the evenings, she returns to the apartment that she shares with Jessica. Every now and then, she passes the small tree she painted on the wall as a child in the Mural Arts program, and she smiles. She has not just endured; she has persevered—and prevailed. ■